GUIDE TO RECOVERY:
A Book For Adult Children of Alcoholics

Herbert L. Gravitz, Ph.D.
Julie D. Bowden, M. S.

With a Foreword by Sharon Wegscheider-Cruse

LP Learning Publications, Inc.
Holmes Beach, Florida

Library of Congress Number: 84-48494

Copyright 1985   Herbert L. Gravitz
                   Julie D. Bowden

Library of Congress Cataloging in Publication Data

Gravitz, Herbert L., 1942-
    Guide to Recovery.

    (Human services library)
    Bibliography: p.
    Includes index.
    1. Alcoholics—United States—Family relationships—Miscellanea.
2. Alcoholism—Treatment—United States—Miscellanea.   3. Adult children—United States—Family relationships—Miscellanea.   I. Bowden, Julie D., 1944-   . II. Title. III. Series.
HV5132.G73   1985   362.2'9286'0973   84-48494
ISBN 0-918452-82-1 (pbk.)

Learning Publications, Inc.
P.O. Box 1326
Holmes Beach, Florida 33509

Softcover: ISBN 0-918452-82-1

Cover Design by Barbara J. Wirtz

Printing: 6 7 8   Year: 6 7 8

Printed and bound in the United States of America

Acknowledgments

Our grateful appreciation goes to our families whose patience, faith, and caring sustained us. To my loving wife of 19 years and my three sons who understood the long hours and weekends required to complete this book. To Dondra, Tony, and Danae—thank you for the consistent encouragement.

Thanks to: Bill B., John M., Linda B., Jerry W., Pam D., Rick U., Suzanne E., and Sue Y.; our first psychotherapy group for "Adult Children of Alcoholics" at the University of California at Santa Barbara in 1981; The Santa Barbara City College Adult Education Program, particularly Ellen Downing for faith in us and the opportunity to work with over 1,500 adult children who taught—and continued to teach—us countless lessons; John Stoddard for encouragement and cheer; Luis Tovar for insightful assistance on minority adult children; Raymond Wilcove for his proof-reading acumen; and Danna Downing for her enthusiastic, negotiable, and humane approach to editing.

Especial thanks go to Linda Mears of Copy Desk for her heroic and talented help. She unselfishly met every difficult deadline we asked. She transcribed our initial tapes and typed on first draft. Without her, this book would have stumbled and stalled.

We also thank our teachers and colleagues on the Board of Directors of the National Association for Children of Alcoholics, who very early expressed faith in our work. We have never seen a finer group of human beings! Dr. Robert Ackerman was especially encouraging and supportive.

Finally, we thank the many others who gave of their time, their heart, and their pain and who are not mentioned by name because of lack of space—not gratitude.

*This book is dedicated to all the
adult children of alcoholics who, in
sharing their lives with us, taught
us what we now offer back.*

Consulting Editor
Human Service Series

Robert J. Ackerman

Table of Contents

Chapter 8 Genesis

A Final Note From The Authors

Appendices

Foreword

We are hearing more and more about adult children of alcoholics, how widespread their identification is becoming, the serious emotional and sometimes physical problems they face, and now how their issues can be addressed. In the last few months, many books have become available in addressing adult children of alcoholics. One of the best is this work by Julie D. Bowden and Herbert L. Gravitz. Their book is written in a clear, concise, easy to read question and answer format. As I travel around the country, I am continually asked questions very similar to the questions raised in this book. It will help me a great deal to be able to refer to their book in order to bring answers, ideas, and new information to the countless numbers of adult children who are so eager for clarity. Clarity of what happened to them and understanding of how to self-help are two very helpful themes that run through Herb and Julie's work. On a personal level, it is comforting and exciting for me to know that Herb and Julie have facilitated countless sessions (personal and group) with adult children and truly know what they are talking about. May you enjoy this book as much as I have and may you enjoy sharing it with your clients and friends.

Sharon Wegscheider-Cruse

1
Introduction

Leslie was mesmerized. The muscles around her eyes tightened as the shock of recognition crossed her face. The stories she was hearing sounded just like hers! The other people in this group, who looked so picture-perfect, had experienced the same abandonment, the same loss of childhood, the same sense of betrayal that she had felt in a home dominated by an alcoholic parent.

Ann, who had recently celebrated her eighty-first birthday, relaxed as she heard others describe the embarrassment of their childhoods—the humiliations, the insults, the times they were afraid to come home, and those terrible holiday scenes. As the shrouds of silence slowly disappeared, she was no longer feeling isolated and alone. There were no secrets here. These were her stories too.

Brian was trembling. He was thinking of his parents. Pangs of guilt pierced his stomach. For the first time he actually talked about what went on in his family. He dared say out loud to others that his parents were alcoholic. He fidgeted as he forced himself not to pretend anymore. But it was hard! Scary! Yet, somewhere at the edge of his awareness, there was a feeling, a real feeling, that he did not want to deny.

Eric felt detached, as if he were a million miles away. He did not like to think about what had happened. He wanted to forget. What was the use anyway? Nothing changes; nothing really makes a difference. If only he could get rid of those recurring nightmares. He barely remembers them in the morning. He just knows they come.

The Leslies, Anns, Brians, Erics, and the millions of others like them, are adult children of alcoholics. Reared in a home in which one or both parents are alcoholic, they are united by the bondage of parental alcoholism. Most adult children of alcoholics have always suspected that something is wrong. They often experience loneliness and they are likely to believe that they are different from other people. They are! Without fully identifying the source of their emptiness, they have endured and suffered. They have survived the experience of living in a family where unpredictability was the one thing that could be counted on. They seldom knew what to expect from parents—a frown or a smile, a slap or a kiss. They have survived the experience of living in a family where inconsistency was the rule. No two days were the same and they could not believe in what others said. Subjected to denial, broken promises, and lies, they were often at the mercy of parents whose feelings, perceptions and judgments were clouded by a mind-altering drug—alcohol. They have survived the experience of living in a family where everything was arbitrary—things were always happening by whim or impulse in ways that seemed out of control. And because their families were like this, they have survived living with a family in chaos. Almost every day there were crises and emergencies at home. It was never really safe to relax—or be a child. Since their families represented their worlds, they lived in a world of unpredictability, inconsistency, arbitrariness, and chaos. These are the children of alcoholics.

This book is for these survivors, the children who grew up in an alcoholic family and became adults. It describes the costs they have had to pay to survive. More important, it presents a way they can re-evaluate their survival techniques in light of the problems they now face as adults. This book will help adult children of alcoholics to use these techniques as resources to propel themselves forward to a life of meaning and joy. As one adult child of an alcoholic said, "If I can use the debris of outrageous misfortune and turn it into something positive, then none of what happened to me occurred without rhyme or reason."

This book reflects recent changes in the field of alcoholism and growing efforts to identify and assist adult children of alcoholics. New and exciting things are happening. It was not until 1955 that alcoholism was recognized as a disease by the American Medical Association.[40] In the 1960s and 1970s it slowly became increasingly clear to professionals that the family develops a parallel disease of its own.[6,33,50,53] And in the late 1970s and early 1980s, explicit acknowledgment has been given to the adult survivors. [8,14,30,58] Then, on Valentine's Day of 1983, the National Association for Children of Alcoholics was formed to recognize the needs and problems of children of alcoholics of all ages.[44] Yes, things are happening!

This book is a part of what is happening. It is about a neglected minority numbering in the millions. Recent estimates indicate there are between 28 and 34 million children of alcoholics, over half of them adults.[7,31]

Because their survival behaviors tend to be approval-seeking and socially acceptable, the problems of most children (and adult children) of alcoholics remain invisible.[46] It is not that they are not being treated. They are—in mental health agencies, psychotherapists' offices, hospitals, employee assistance programs, and the judicial system.[44] But the importance of their parents' alcoholism often does not receive the focus and attention it merits. Despite the increasing recognition of alcoholism as a family disease, children of alcoholics continue to be ignored, misdiagnosed, and inappropriately treated. Many limp into adulthood behind a facade of strength. They survive adulthood, too, but do not enjoy it.

This is a book about how children of alcoholics of all ages can begin to enjoy their adult lives. We want to share what we have been learning from the adult children of alcoholics we have encountered as therapists and educators. Most of all we want to share our enthusiasm and excitement as well as convey a message of hope and understanding. We have seen dramatic, positive changes in adult children of alcoholics once they understand how their earlier experience with familial alcoholism continues to influence them.

We invite you to join us on a journey in which we are all pioneers. The journey will help you to uncover the influence of family alcoholism. The approach we will use is a question and answer format. The questions addressed are those we have been asked most frequently by adult children of alcoholics. As we have journeyed with others, we have come to appreciate that there will be a number of responses to what is discovered. Some people are surprised, shocked, or overwhelmed by the answers. Some become angry and frustrated. Others remain skeptical and want to know where the "research" is. Some become very sad and cry, while others feel relief, elation, and hope. Few remain unaffected. There are reasons for the strong emotional responses provoked by the questions and answers presented in this book.

First and foremost, we will be talking about all those things that children of alcoholics of all ages are taught *not* to talk about. One of the cardinal rules in an alcoholic home is, "There's nothing wrong here and don't you dare tell anybody!"[8,53] So we are most reverently breaking the shroud of silence that encases the alcoholic family. We dare to discuss things as they are, not as they should be or as you might like them to be. We know alcoholism is one of the most prevalent diseases;[38] one in three families are affected.[26] The alcoholic family is "the family next door." Alcoholism is also a complex and puzzling disease; we still do not know exactly what causes it.[52] We know it is a devastating disease. It affects the body, mind, and spirit.[37] It affects the individual, family, and society.[38] It is generational. And because it is generational it affects the future.[27] There are almost 15 million Americans suffering from alcoholism or problem drinking. Their numbers are increasing by almost half a million people each year. Over 75 million Americans are affected and alcoholism costs this country over $120 billion a year.[55] Every two and one-half minutes there is an alcohol related death.[15]

Second, adult children of alcoholics are profoundly affected when they overcome the barrier of denial because this requires them to confront the consequences of this ravaging disease in a very personal way. Children of alcoholics are at maximum risk of becoming alcoholic themselves or developing other addictive behavior. They are at the risk of marrying an alcoholic, one or several times. And they are at the risk of developing predictable problematic patterns of behavior in which they get stuck over and over again. [8,19,26] Yet most do not even understand what hit them. There is no such thing as growing up unaffected when alcoholism is present in a family, but it is difficult for the individual to acknowledge these problems. Arrested emotional development is inescapable unless the effects of this disease are dealt with. Alcohol is an equal opportunity destroyer. Whoever gets in its path is affected.

Third, a multitude of powerful feelings is provoked when the individual begins to come to terms with the past. Over and over we have seen adult children experience spontaneous age regression. This means that as adult children break the denial and silence, they find themselves thrown back to the past. Particular words, music, or places trigger memories from childhood. Some of these experiences have not been remembered or felt in years. Some are pleasant; many are not. All are real. Remembering and exploring the effects of growing up with alcoholism in the family is part of a larger process of learning, growth, and development. In other words, this is a journey of change. And change is always scary. No matter how miserable you are, at least your life is predictable as it is. Adult children of alcoholics often confuse stability with consistency and rigidly cling to what is familiar even though it is destructive.

Adult children of alcoholics already know much of what we shall discuss. They just do not know that they know! Our task is to make this knowledge more accessible, meaningful, and useful. We believe that in each of us there is a core of wisdom and strength. The human mind has more resources than it can possibly use. It is a vast territory of undiscovered potential. We believe people make the best choices they can with the information they have and that with new information they will make better choices. While this means our parents made the best choices they could, it does not mean that they did not make terrible mistakes at times. We believe that people grow best in an atmosphere of freedom and choice; that people with the most choices are usually the healthiest and happiest. Sometimes adult children of alcoholics are so eager to change that they will reject valuable parts of themselves. Yet there is a positive aspect to almost every part of us if we can just find the right context for its expression.

In reading this book, you may find that your experiences do not match everything that is described. Use this material as a place to begin. Take what is helpful and leave the rest. We could not possibly cover everything and we have probably left out some questions that are important to you. Begin to trust the validity of your own experiences, knowing you will make sense out of our words and find your own meaning. It is up to you to decide what kind of changes you want to make, if any, and how this book can best serve your needs. You can decide, for instance, how much of this book to read, when to read it, and with whom to share it. Sometimes the best way to move quickly is to go slowly! Honor your own pace and speed. It has been our experience that the book works best when read in sequence. However, maximum benefit will come if you also feel free to put the book down at times. Taking a walk, talking to a friend, developing a support system, or going to Al-Anon can help you get through difficult sections. Reading the book when you are under the influence of alcohol or other drugs will not be helpful.

Finally, this book provides a way to share the questions and experiences of adult children of alcoholics. Together, we will explore the inner workings of an alcoholic family. We will discover what roles the children adopt and how these bear on their adult lives. We will look at the personal and interpersonal difficulties in which adult children frequently become enmeshed. We will also talk about what can be done to overcome these difficulties and describe the recovery process. We will show that traumatic incidents in childhood can lead to abilities and personal strengths that the individual can draw upon during the recovery process. We will see how strength can be restored from wounding. We shall discover new paths to freedom.

So we welcome you on what we anticipate will be a most important journey—your journey, your recovery. It is time!

2
Roots

1. What is an adult child of an alcoholic?

The phrase "adult children of alcoholics" was used by a few alcoholism professionals in the 1970s when research and clinical observation began to demonstrate that children growing up in families where there is alcoholism are particularly vulnerable.[9,18,59] They are susceptible to certain emotional, physical, and spiritual problems.[8,19,48,55] The National Association for Children of Alcoholics considers adult children of alcoholics as having an adjustment reaction to familial alcoholism which is recognizable, diagnosable, and treatable.[44] Based on our work, we consider an adult child of an alcoholic to be anyone who comes from a family (either the family of origin or the family of adoption) where alcohol abuse was a primary and central issue. We have found that almost everyone who has an alcoholic parent has been and is profoundly affected by the experience.

Mental health professionals have encountered adult children of alcoholics by the millions, but have not accurately diagnosed the roots of their complaints. Children of alcoholics appear for treatment for a host of reasons other than for being children of alcoholics. For example, they are treated for alcoholism, co-alcoholism, eating disorders, learning disabilities, depression, and severe stress. Until recently, explicit acknowledgment has not been given to their plight as children of alcoholics. It is time to identify them more meaningfully. It is time to call them adult children of alcoholics. To do so is an important step in uncovering the nature of their difficulties and providing effective interventions. It initiates recovery!

Some people are not sure whether their parents are or were suffering from alcoholism. We have found that if the question is there, then it is likely the problem is there. It is very similar to asking, "Am I an alcoholic?" If I am asking that question, chances are I am an alcoholic.

2. What is an alcoholic?

There are many ways to define alcoholism. The strict, most literal description of an alcoholic is someone who is physically addicted to the drug alcohol; that is, when you remove the drug, the person goes into withdrawal.[37,40] If there is a physical withdrawal process (which might include sweating, trembling, anxiety or hallucinations), then you have an advanced alcoholic.[55] However, we consider this a rather limited view because it ignores the psychological implications and addresses the disease only after it has progressed to late stages. Instead, we use a simple model to determine if someone is an alcoholic. A person is alcoholic if he or she: 1) drinks, 2) gets into trouble repeatedly as a result of drinking—be that trouble with family, career, work, health, or the law—and 3) continues to drink. If somebody drinks, gets into trouble, and drinks again, repeating the cycle over and over, we consider that person an alcoholic.

Alcoholism is a devastating, potentially fatal disease. The primary symptom of having it is telling everyone—including yourself—that you are not an alcoholic.

No one sets out to lose control and thereby become an alcoholic. Alcoholism develops subtly and insidiously. If untreated, alcoholism becomes progressively worse.

Alcoholics drink not because they are depressed, not because they are scared, not because they are sad, not because they are happy. They drink because they no longer have a choice. They have lost control.[37,40,52]

3. Why is alcoholism called a family disease?

This is one of the new developments in the field of alcoholism and family therapy. As mentioned earlier, it was only in the 1950s that alcoholism was recognized as a disease, though tens of millions had died from it. In the 1960s it was suggested that people intimately involved with the alcoholic may *also* have a disease—a parallel disease. This disease was later referred to as "co-alcoholism" or "co-dependency."[30,53] It was observed that the spouse of the alcoholic is drawn into the disease process.[22,57] In the 1970s and 1980s it became increasingly clear to professionals that other family members, too, are seriously affected by the alcoholic.

As the alcoholic becomes sicker and sicker, there is a parallel breakdown in his or her family. As the alcoholic loses more and more control, others in the family adapt by assuming increasing amounts of responsibility. Someone begins to do those things the alcoholic is not doing. Someone makes excuses to friends and family. In this way, alcohol reaches beyond its chemical effects on the individual abuser and becomes a family affair. The family's demoralization is as devastating as the alcoholism itself.

Initially, the family is not aware of what is happening. Like the alcoholic, family members do not want to face the reality of their situation. Their denial becomes a hallmark in the same way that denial is a hallmark of alcoholism. It seemingly protects them from the terror of acknowledging that their lives are out of control. The family is no longer a safe place in which to communicate, to grow, or to love. Implicit rules guide the family along a path of sickness and, at times, destruction. Family members easily begin to develop unhealthy ways of coping with family life.

4. What is a home like when there is an active alcoholic in the family?

In a home where one or both parents are actively alcoholic, family life has a distinctive character. Family life is *inconsistent, unpredictable, arbitrary, and chaotic*[10,29] These four words typify life in an alcoholic family. For example, what is true one day may not be true the next day. A child may have a conversation with a drunken parent one night, but when the child refers to it later, the parent may have absolutely no recollection of that conversation. In an alcoholic "blackout" a person experiences a type of chemical amnesia and cannot remember what was said or done. The child does not understand what has happened. Even alcoholic parents may not realize they have experienced a blackout. That is one reason life is so inconsistent and unpredictable. Another is that personalities change with alcoholism. For example, if I am the child of an alcoholic, my mother might be the most loving, wonderful woman when she is sober, but just the opposite when she is drinking. I cannot be sure which person I am going to meet when I come home. Children of alcoholics learn specific lessons from this. They learn to repress spontaneity, to first check things out to see if their parents are sober, and how to shrug off disappointment. There is a whole set of behaviors and attitudes a child develops and carries into adult life as a result of such lessons.

The arbitrariness stems from the whimsical and impulsive changes that occur from one day to the next; and, of course, children are unable to determine the basis for these changes. They cannot understand that the arbitrariness stems from the alcohol abuse. For example, very often parents are unable to agree on rules for their children. If I am a child of an alcoholic, it might be that this week my parents have decided that I am old enough to go out and stay out as late as I want. Next week, for no apparent reason, I am not allowed out of the house. Or, my father might have a rule that says I cannot date until I am 18. My mother decides that this is too harsh. She believes I should have much more freedom. So I have two conflicting rules.

So much in the alcoholic home is arbitrary, unpredictable and inconsistent because everything is based on a drug which impairs functioning. Chaos is the natural result. Include in this picture the certain emotional abuse, as well as the potential for physical or sexual abuse and you can see that life in an alcoholic home is like living with an accident every day.

5. What is a "normal" home like?

This question is often asked by adult children of alcoholics. There is no such thing as a "normal" home. Unfortunately, children of alcoholics often believe that somewhere, somehow, there exists a perfect family. This notion of the perfect family is the standard against which they judge their own family life. They have unreasonable expectations with which they compare themselves unmercifully. It appears to them that everyone else is happy and well adjusted while they are different and damaged.

Let us say that a "normal" family is simply one without alcoholism or where members can talk openly about their experiences. However, instead of looking at things in terms of normal or abnormal, it is more useful to think in terms of functional and dysfunctional. Functional homes promote children's sense of well-being; they are relatively consistent, somewhat predictable, minimally arbitrary, and only occasionally chaotic. In terms of family roles, there is appropriate delegation of authority. Youngsters are not expected to drive cars, or do the grocery shopping, or run the household. Children are not given the responsibilities of parenting. The parents are not children and the children are not the parents.

Rules are more explicit in functional families.[53] They do not change from day to day or from hour to hour, so children usually know what is expected from them. However, the rules parents make tend to be flexible and suited to particular situations. Parents generally allow input from the children about how they view rules. Rules tend to be realistic, humane, and not impossible to follow.

The rules take into account the unique feelings, beliefs, and differences of family members. When feelings are expressed, they are listened to and accepted. Children are heard and treated with respect in a functional family. There are rules that state: "Don't be violent; don't be abusive, cruel, or mean. Tell us what is wrong so we can help." It is also permissible to be separate, have your own things, and your own identity. Boundaries between each individual are accepted, encouraged, and respected. Communications tend to be open instead of closed. When communications are open, one can talk to others about what they think is happening. For example, if my mom falls off her chair at the dinner table, I can say, "Hey, mom fell off her chair . . . What's happening? . . . I'm scared . . . What can we do?" In a closed, alcoholic system the rules say, "Don't talk. Don't trust. Don't feel."[8]

In a functional family children depend on adults. Children trust that they will be cared for. They are allowed to be children and they know it will be that way tomorrow, too. In a functional home children are taught how to cope and how to assume responsibility. New roles are not thrust upon them in one drunken weekend, but are conveyed over years of nurturing. They will not suddenly be expected to take on parental tasks for which they are not prepared when a parent vanishes into a bottle or disappears to a bar.

Children do not live in fear in a functional family. In too many alcoholic homes, children live in fear because of the abuse to which they are subjected. Common fears are that they will be hurt or abandoned, that they are unlovable, and that things are out of control. This is a result of the parents not being emotionally and physically available. In a functional family children know there is someone more resourceful than themselves. In a functional family children know they will not be abandoned regardless of what they do. In an alcoholic home the child feels abandoned again and again. As one adult child of an alcoholic said, "When I was a little child, my parents abandoned me, and they never left the house."

Still, functional families are human; they are not perfect. That is important to know. In a functional family there may be yelling and screaming—but not typically. There may be anxiety and tension—but not on a daily basis. There may be unhappiness—but not usually. And there may be anger and hurt—but it is not chronic.

6. Does it make a difference how old I was when my parent(s) became alcoholic or if they left home when I was a child?

What seems to be true is that the negative effects of having lived in an alcoholic family are greater the younger the child is as the disease progresses and the longer he or she lives with an alcoholic parent.[1,21,39] So yes, we believe it does make a difference how old the child is. And if the alcoholic parent leaves home, there will be some difference in effects, but the child must deal with literal abandonment issues and is then often raised by a co-alcoholic who is sick also. It has been said that the only difference between the alcoholic and the co-alcoholic is that one does not drink.[33] In other respects, this parent engages in many of the same behaviors that undermine the child's sense of safety and well-being.

7. What if both parents are alcoholic?

Research suggests that if you have two alcoholic parents, you are going to be younger the first time you get drunk, you are going to have more behavioral problems before you get into a treatment program, and the period between the first intoxication and treatment is going to be much shorter. You will also tend to develop alcoholism much more rapidly.[39] Common sense would also suggest that with both parents alcoholic, the child has even fewer resources available than if one parent was sober. It is getting both barrels of the shotgun, so to speak. Neither parent is available in any consistent, meaningful, protective way. So, children who have two alcoholic parents have an even more difficult time and are even more susceptible and more vulnerable to all the problems affecting children of alcoholics. Recent research supports the idea that children with two alcoholic parents have a greater genetic sensitivity to alcohol and, if alcohol abuse occurs, to develop alcoholism more rapidly.[34]

8. How does all this apply to me if my parents were addicted to drugs other than alcohol?

Much of it applies, depending on what other drugs we are talking about. Alcohol happens to be the number one drug of choice in many cultures;

it is legal, very acceptable, and easily accessible. Children reared by parents who are addicted to illegal drugs have all of the problems and concerns of children reared in homes where alcohol is abused. They also have one additional problem—the illegality of the substance abused and the corresponding need for duplicity, breaking the law, and concealing information. In addition there is the fact that parents who deal with illegal drugs are also more prone to deal with unsavory people and to be in violent situations. For instance, if we are talking about a drug like cocaine, people can become so financially indebted to their dealer that physical threats or actual physical violence may occur.

Prescription drugs can be very similar to alcohol in that they are quite acceptable. Again, we have a very insidious drug about which some physicians may say, "It's all right to take this, Mrs. Jason. Go ahead and refill it whenever you need to." Only when the patient or the addict begins lying to get more prescriptions or when the mood swings are extreme is it no longer acceptable. Often the family does not know what it is dealing with because nobody sees the drug being used. Valium and similar drugs are also less toxic to the human body than alcohol; the user may therefore appear outwardly more healthy than an alcoholic.[56] Yet, if you have a mother who is up and down on Valium and "speed" under a doctor's orders, you may have some crazy situations that are just as unpredictable, just as inconsistent, just as arbitrary, and just as chaotic as those with an alcoholic parent.

9. Do all adult children of alcoholics feel the same?

Although children of alcoholics each have a different perspective and see the environment, their parents, and their situation from their own vantage point, we consistently find that they identify with certain general experiences. Often after we have described the "typical childhood" of an adult child of an alcoholic in a class, someone will approach us and say, "Everything you said sounded like you were talking about me." Most develop similar feelings and fears. It is a relief for many to discover that they are not alone.

Nevertheless, not all children of alcoholics experience identical emotional and physical effects. A number of variables account for this beyond the fact that each and every child is unique. Again, one factor is the child's age at the onset of parental alcoholism. Another is whether one or both parents are alcoholics. Other factors include the following: whether it is the mother or the father who is alcoholic; the number of children in the family; birth order; whether the spouse is working on his or her recovery; whether or not there are other, helpful influences available, such as family, friends and teachers; and whether or not there is physical or sexual abuse. Further, external factors such as the family's socioeconomic status may affect the child of an alcoholic.[1]

Even in the same family not all children will react the same way. For example, one child may clearly see the alcoholism, while another may not consider it a problem. In fact, he or she might get quite upset with the sibling for even insinuating that alcohol is a problem in their family. Many adult children of alcoholics have told us that when they spoke to another family member about alcoholism in the home, the other reacted with disbelief, saying, "What alcoholism? Who was an alcoholic? Dad wasn't an alcoholic!" Sometimes they encounter very hostile responses from siblings and a great deal of anger for "maligning" a parent. One child in the family might remember a series of horrors in childhood, while a brother or sister might choose to remember only the good times and wonders, "Why do you dig up all those ugly things?" While each child in a family may find his or her unique way to adapt to the situation, all will exhibit difficulties in feeling emotion and trusting themselves or others.

10. Why do I feel so strange, confused, and scared?

We have been describing a family atmosphere that is almost certain to cause a child to feel inadequate, tense, and upset. It seems impossible to grow up in this kind of environment without feelings of confusion, guilt, anger, shame, or fear. These are "normal" responses to an "abnormal" situation. It is no wonder that you feel strange, confused, and scared! If you are the adult child of an alcoholic, you grew up in a family where there was a family disease, a family secret, and shared but unacknowledged family pain.

11. When did all this begin?

The effects of alcoholism actually began before your birth. They began with the development of the personalities of parents who are themselves often children of alcoholics and still traumatized when they become parents. If parents consume enough alcohol, it can affect the unborn child.[17] The chances of being affected by fetal alcohol syndrome (FAS) are high for children whose mothers drink heavily during pregnancy. The genetic, biochemical, and neurophysiological mechanisms involved in alcoholism may begin to affect the child at the moment of conception.[19,40,48,52] This is in addition to the environmental impact we have been describing. Since heredity and environment have an impact on the development of the child, the effects of parental alcoholism begin very early in the child's life, long before he or she is aware that there is a problem.

12. Where does this leave the children of alcholics?

Children of alcholics have acquired biological and psychological vulnerabilities that follow them into adulthood and which, if not addressed, can become a permanent disability.[9,18,20,59] It is as though the child has been wounded and was never properly treated. Like an injury not allowed to heal properly, it carries over into adulthood as a chronic health problem.

Yet, what we have found particularly exciting and what makes us optimistic is that children of alcoholics have learned to cope with a variety of truly difficult, sometimes life-threatening situations. In the face of stress and trauma they have learned to survive. This same strength can be drawn upon to recover from the negative effects of parental alcoholism.

3
Survival

13. Why are adult children of alcoholics called "survivors"?

This term acknowledges that adult children of alcoholics made it through childhood, and stayed alive in what could be described as a war zone. Like shell-shocked war veterans, there were many times throughout their childhoods when their lives were threatened—emotionally and spiritually as well as physically. Some were sexually violated. Children of alcoholics do an amazing job of dodging, negotiating, hiding, learning, and adapting just to stay alive. They learn to be survivors despite the demand that they pretend there is nothing wrong. They have had to shut down their own emotional life many times. They learned to deny it, block it out, repress it, isolate it, dissociate from it. Otherwise, their feelings could have overwhelmed them. Terribly traumatic things happen to children of alcoholics. And it is a testament to their skill and courage that they arrive at adulthood.

Children of alcoholics had to survive essentially alone, because that is the nature of the disease of alcoholism. It is an isolating, separating, and lonely disease. Most of these children had to suffer in silence. They thought nobody would believe what they said even if they would dare say it. Who could believe it? In fact, they probably had the experience of being told in no uncertain terms not to speak about what was happening. In the classroom it may have been clear to them that talking about such issues with the teacher was not acceptable. They may have known relatives who watched what was happening and did not speak up. There was a secret, a shroud of silence everywhere.[13] Nobody would speak. No one would acknowledge the obvious. One woman we worked with spent a great deal of time dealing with her anger—and later all the hurt—at the adult relatives around her who saw that her parents were alcoholic, that she was being abused, that she was very troubled, and still did not reach out to help her. They said nothing. She felt betrayed.

So adult children of alcoholics are called survivors because they have been through a war—and made it. If they are alive and reading this book, we know they made it through. We know that they can, have, and will survive.

14. I feel like I was never a kid. What happened to my childhood?

This is an experience that children of alcoholics very often report. They are right when they say, "I was never a kid." They really did not experience the freedom and the carefree years of childhood. They were too busy surviving, placating, picking up the pieces, adjusting, and being responsible. In other words, they were too busy being everything but a child.

In an alcoholic family, as the alcoholism progresses and co-alcoholism develops, there really is very little time left for the children to be children. They are not treated as children, and may even come to have difficulty seeing themselves as children. Children need a certain availability and a certain responsiveness from parents who are not often present in an alcoholic family.[8] Many times the children are instead required to be available and responsive to the parents' needs. Children are vulnerable and rely upon their parents to take care of them, to protect them. However, in an alcoholic family it is not safe for children to be children. Often there is no one there to take care of them. To cope with the situation and hide the fear of having no one to turn to, children of alcoholics learn to build a facade of strength and competence. They learn to act like an adult while they are still children.

An eight-year-old girl we worked with described how frightened she became when she heard a fight starting between her parents after she had gone to sleep. As the shouting increased and other sounds mounted (glass breaking, slapping), she made her little sister move to her bed. Over the smaller child's weeping, she reassured her, "It's all right. Daddy won't hurt Mommy, and they'll make up. Everything will be fine, just you wait and see." She set aside her own terror to parent her sister. The following day she continued this pseudo-adult role by taking care of her mother and offering to help with household chores, while reassuring her that everything would be fine.

Another child lived in a home where the alcoholism was less obvious. His father, while not a stumbling drunk, was not available in any consistent or predictable way. The boy loved him very much and did not want to be a burden. Since he often could not be sure whether his father was drunk, he devised a test. When his father came home, he would challenge him to a game of basketball. If his father lost, the son knew he had been drinking and there would be a long night ahead. If his father won, then he was sober and the evening would be safe.

We know another child who would be invited to play at a neighbor's house, yet never felt free to say, "Sure, I can do that. I don't have to do anything until dinner." Rather, the child was very aware of a need to go home at the end of the school day to check on everything that was happening. The child needed to know who was sober, who was there and whether or not she would be needed to care for the other children or start preparing the family dinner.

All of these children had their childhood usurped by premature adulthood. Typically, there is a reversal of parent and child roles. This means that the children really never had a chance to play and have fun, never really had a chance to be free of the shackles of all that responsibility, guilt, worry, and caretaking. Many children of alcoholics, by the time they reach their late adolescent and early adult years, are already burned out—weary from being an adult for the first 20 years of their life.

15. What happens when children are raised in a home where it is forbidden to talk openly about what is happening in the family?

First and foremost, children are taught to disown what their eyes see and what their ears hear. Because of denial in the family, children's perceptions of what is happening become progressively and systematically negated. Overtly or covertly, explicitly or implicitly, they are told not to believe what their own senses tell them. As a result, the children learn to distrust their own experience. At the same time, they are taught not to trust other people. How can it be otherwise when they are actually observing one thing while the significant adults around them are telling them another. For example, a boy may see his alcoholic mother fall off her chair at the dinner table and not get up. His stomach muscles tighten, he gasps for breath, and starts reaching for her because he senses she needs help. His father, with a glaring look from across the table, insists that there is nothing wrong. His look says nothing happened and not to move. "Mother is fine," he states. "Leave her alone, ignore her, and go on eating." So the child sits carefully at the table with tears beginning to run down his cheeks as his mother struggles to get up. He tells himself to be quiet, to pretend nothing unusual is happening, and he tells his throat, tight from the tears, to swallow that next bite of food.

This child is being taught many lessons. He is learning that his judgment is poor and incorrect. "Nothing is wrong," he is told, but everything seems wrong. "I must be misperceiving. I must be wrong," he starts thinking, "because how could my father deny my mother help if she really needs it?" The child learns to tolerate many intolerable situations. After all, the child concludes, "I am not seeing it right. I do not understand what is happening. Maybe I should just accept the situation." The child learns that his natural responses are somehow unacceptable, wrong, not to be trusted. The child also learns that at least one of these adults is lying to him or telling him something that goes totally against everything he is sensing, everything that his experience tells him is real. Ultimately, the child is taught not to trust himself or others. The results are disastrous.[11]

When people learn at an early age not to trust experience and not to trust body signals, they begin to ignore feelings. When the boy in our example sat at the table and his mom fell to the floor in the middle of a meal, and he was told to sit there and eat, he learned still another lesson. He learned to set aside a whole set of important feelings and continue on through mealtime, or through another experience, or through life, just as if nothing had happened. To do that, he had to separate from his feelings. So, 20 years later, he may be sitting with a friend or in therapy talking about mealtimes at his home when he was a child. And he might say that when he was nine-years-old, mealtimes were pretty interesting, because his family would be eating and his mom would fall off her chair. And he might describe this with a calm voice and a stilted smile. He might tell you this with absolutely no sense of the feelings that initially accompanied that experience. In fact, the feelings are there, but he has been taught to keep them separate. As a result, he never learned how to fully integrate his feelings, thoughts, and observations.

A child who is not allowed to talk openly about the alcoholism in the family begins to think there is something wrong with him or her. He or she feels confused, scared, bad, sick or crazy. And there can be no discussion of the situation and no explanation that such feelings are common when you live with an alcoholic.

16. What are the rules that implicitly or explicitly guide an alcoholic family?

Three primary rules are described by Claudia Black, in her pioneering work with children of alcoholics.[8] The rules that she found over and over are, "Don't talk, don't trust, don't feel." Sharon Wegscheider-Cruse, another pioneer who has written extensively about the alcoholic family, notes that the rules in an alcoholic home tend to be unhealthy, inhuman and rigid.[53] She describes the alcoholic's use of alcohol as the issue around which everything else is centered. No other issue affects the family so deeply. Yet family rules state that alcohol is *not* the cause of family problems; someone or something else is at fault; alcoholism is not the problem. Additionally, the *status quo* must be maintained at all costs, and everyone must take over the alcoholic's responsibilities, cover up, protect, accept the rules and not rock the boat. No one may talk about what is going on to anyone else, and no one may say what he or she is really feeling. To abide by these rules is to be safe; to break these rules is to court disaster.

We find that two different sets of rules occur. One set consists of rules the parents give to the child. These rules are built on domination, fear, guilt, and shame. We have already talked about those. Another set of rules is developed by the child in response to the parents' rules. They go something like this: "If I don't talk, nobody will know how I feel, and I won't get hurt. If I don't ask, I can't get rejected. If I'm invisible, I'll be okay. If I'm careful, no one will get upset. If I stop feeling, I won't have any pain." The prime directive becomes, "I must make things as safe as possible." But "safety" can exact a heavy price.

17. What impact does this family atmosphere and these rules have upon the children?

In the midst of an atmosphere of unpredictability, inconsistency, arbitrariness, and chaos, the children try to make sense out of what is happening. When placed in such an unstable world, they begin to think that they are unstable and that the instability in the family is their fault. If you could listen to what the child cannot say, you might hear something like this: "This is crazy, so I must be crazy. Something's wrong so there must be something wrong with me. I haven't got love, so I must be unlovable."

Then further translations occur. "I must be unlovable" becomes "I don't need love." "I don't need love," becomes "I don't want love." "I don't want love," becomes "I will reject love when it comes because there is no such thing; I cannot trust it, it's not safe!" So, "I don't need love, I don't want love," ultimately become "I won't take love. I can't take it!"

It is easy to forget how profound the parent-child relationship is. Children are completely dependent upon their parents' good will and nurturing. Parents are the people who make it possible, literally, to stay alive. They provide the home. They provide the food. Parents are also a primary source of a child's sense of self worth. When the people who love them the most hurt them the most, children often conclude that there must be something dreadfully wrong with them. "I must be bad, sick, or crazy." In this way, children of alcoholics learn to distrust both themselves and others. They learn to endure, to suffer, and to resent. They survive by distancing themselves from their feelings and denying their needs. Feelings and needs are too dangerous, too painful. Instead, children in families of alcoholics learn to control; they learn to pretend or to lie or both. As a result, they learn to blur, distort, and confuse.[30] Love becomes confused with caretaking, spontaneity with irrationality, intimacy with smothering, anger with violence. Just as alcoholics blur their view of the world due to alcohol, children blur the boundaries of feelings, thoughts, and behaviors due to the alcoholism of the parents.

Often a child is explicitly told by a parent, "You are the reason why I'm feeling this way. . .why I'm drinking. . .why I'm this. . .why I'm that. It's your fault. If only you. . ." Children are wonderfully self-centered. All young children tend to think that they are the center of the universe; so it is very natural for them to incorporate these immensely powerful statements or suggestions by the parent. When told something often enough, we believe it. The children of alcoholics often do believe they are the cause of the problems in the family, and therefore feel they should be able to cure or control the situation. That need for control follows them through life.

18. How do children adjust to this very repressive environment?

Research from the field of family therapy shows that family members adopt identifiable role behaviors when they are under stress. And all alcoholic families are under stress. These roles are adopted both to save the family and to save the child. Virginia Satir, a noted pioneer in family therapy, first described these roles for distressed families in general.[5]

More recently, both Claudia Black and Sharon Wegscheider-Cruse, a student of Satir, separately described common roles specific to alcoholic families.[8,53]

Black's initial work came from her observations of the children of alcoholics seen in inpatient treatment programs.[6,7] She noticed that although most of them seemed to have adjusted quite well on the surface, they did not seem to feel. While there are certainly many overtly problematic children from alcoholic homes, the majority are so busy looking good, so busy people-pleasing, that they are overlooked and ignored. In addition to the "acting-out" or delinquent child, most children adopt one or a combination of the following three roles: the *responsible one*, the *adjuster*, and the *placater*.

The "responsible one" is usually the first-born and often the only child. This child's behavior is organized around the principle, "In the midst of chaos, I'll do it and take care of it." This is the child who begins to pick up responsibilities left behind by a trail of alcoholism and co-alcoholism. These children typically are the marvel of the neighborhood—up very early, to bed very late and, in between, doing everything that needs to be done to run the household. Mature and reliable beyond their years, these children will set their own alarm clocks for the morning, get their younger sisters and brothers up, and make sure that the other children get breakfast. They may even be the ones who are in charge of getting their parents up for work. They are the children who will come home, fix dinner, and then do laundry. They are like the child Black described who had seven sheets of paper along the wall in her room outlining her duties every hour of the day, including one specific hour to relax and play. The child was so responsible that, amid everything else, she also knew she was a child and should play. So that was scheduled in, too. This is a child who does very well in school, and does not come to anybody's attention as having problems. In fact, these children are often seen as very good, very well-adjusted. This might be the teenager who stays after class with her English teacher to help grade papers, who helps other children with projects during class hours, who hands in her paper early. This accomplishes several goals. Not only does the child represent the family positively to the community, she also acquires a sense of stability and control in one area of her life.

The second role is one Black refers to as "the adjuster." The adjuster's guiding thought is, "In the midst of chaos, I'll ignore it." For example, this is the child who seems impervious to the effects of the environment, and he or she adjusts or adapts by detaching. This is the child who sits at the dinner table, watches his mother fall from her seat and seems not to notice, continuing to eat without missing a single bite. This child can sit in a room watching TV while there is screaming going on and continue with whatever he or she is doing no matter what is happening, apparently oblivious to the environment. The neighbors or the parents might say, "How wonderful that Aaron doesn't seem to be affected by the problems at home." Or the teacher might say, "Aaron? Who is Aaron? Oh! He is the quiet kid who sits in the back of the room and never says anything." These children can go through many situations, even an entire school year, and not be noticed. They adjust so well; they make so little noise that it is easy to completely miss them. These are the children who will go along with any and every suggestion because they seem unwilling or incapable of making decisions. They will shrug their shoulders and say, "It doesn't matter," since they have no sense of their own needs. Somewhere along the line they lose that sense of power and self through a belief that they cannot affect their environment or their own lives.

The third role Black calls "the placater." The placater's guiding principle is, "In the midst of chaos, I'll fix it and make it better." What placaters fix are people's feelings, worries, troubles. They learn to be so sensitive and perceptive to what is happening that they can walk into a room, and without even consciously realizing it, figure out just what the level of tension is, who is fighting with whom, and whether it is safe or dangerous. And reflexively they begin to diffuse whatever tension is in the room. Placaters are excellent conflict resolvers and negotiators. They work hard at taking care of everyone's feelings and needs—everyone's except their own. Placaters are typically their parents' marriage counselors at age five. They seem to have been born with a master's degree in social work. When mom and dad are fighting, the placater does something to reduce the tension. When dad comes home from a hard day, this child might meet her father at the door, take his hand and lead him to his favorite chair as she quickly explains, "Mama's not feeling well. She's upstairs lying down. Dinner's in the oven. Don't worry about anything. She'll be just fine later; so let's just go ahead and eat." At school they are Mr. or Ms. Congeniality. Often among the most popular kids in the class, they seldom have an enemy in the world because they are continually pleasing, pleasing, pleasing. The only thing that you might notice is that at least a dozen times each day they say, "Excuse me! I'm sorry! I didn't mean to do that." They even apologize for apologizing.

Wegscheider-Cruse describes the adjustments made by children of alcoholics from a different vantage point.[53] She uses different terms for some of the same roles and includes a fourth one. The oldest daughter or son usually assumes the role of the "hero." The hero provides self-worth for the family with hard work, success, and achievement. He or she will show everyone that the family is all right. The hero will make up for the family's weakness. He or she is admired and respected, but feels like a failure and inadequate. The hero is similar to Black's responsible child. The second child in the family often ends up playing another role, the "scapegoat," which corresponds to the delinquent or acting-out child Black mentions. The scapegoat takes the focus off the family problem of alcoholism by running away, failing, stealing, drinking, or using other drugs. He or she appears consumed with anger, but the characteristic feeling is hurt. By the time the third child comes along, a child who makes no demands is needed. Enter the "lost child" (similar to Black's "adjuster"), who contributes by not being a problem. He or she makes no demands and becomes a loner, preferring privacy to the family's chaos. The lost child spends a lot of time in his or her room, playing alone, and feeling lonely in the role of the forgotten child. This child tends to be shy, withdrawn, and quiet. There is little expected from him or her. Wegscheider-Cruse's last role, the "mascot," is usually assigned to a latecomer, most often the youngest child. The mascot is similar to the placating child, although much more of a clown and a goof-off. Rather than resolving and helping people to work through their feelings, the mascot will typically alleviate the tension by doing something funny. His or her charge is to distract in order to diffuse. The price, however, is high. Immaturity, hyperactivity, fragility, and emotional impoverishment are the result.

With these roles in place, the family is destined to repeat its own history. Each member has his or her own unique function to sustain, reinforcing the unhealthiness in other members as well as in the family as a whole. These roles are progressive, too. This means that they become more rigid and encompassing unless they are interrupted. As we will see, the responsible child becomes the responsible adult, the adjuster child becomes the adjuster adult, and the placating child becomes the placating adult.

It is also true that children from other kinds of dysfunctional families take on similar roles. However, children from alcoholic families have a rigidity about these roles. Unlike other troubled families, the pervasive denial in the alcoholic family deters anyone from talking about what is happening.[1,13] Because of this rigidity and denial, there is little chance to change the situation.

19. I think I have played every one of those roles. Can a person play more than one role?

Yes. As your experience has already told you, children can learn more than one role; they can go through the roles sequentially and sometimes they will exchange roles. We have often heard an only child joke about having to assume all of these different roles at one time or another. Sometimes, when the hero or the responsible child leaves the home, a child who had another role—perhaps as the scapegoat—finally gets a chance to take on the hero role. Children can also trade roles over the years.

20. I am very successful and seem to have a good life; yet, I feel empty and unhappy. What is wrong with me?

What is wrong is that you are the child of an alcoholic, but probably have not yet realized and fully acknowledged the meaning of that experience or the power of that pain. Like many children of alcoholics, you have severed the connection between the alcoholism in your family of origin and the feelings and problems that you are having now. Becoming an adult and moving away (the "geographic cure") does not erase what you learned in that family. The lessons you learned in childhood—for better or worse— tend to endure. There exists in the present an eternal yesterday.

Maybe you have established a brand new family, a family in which there is a real opportunity for intimacy, warmth, trust, and caring. But, unfortunately, all you can see and expect—without realizing it—is another war zone. Reacting out of reflex, you respond to the current situation as if it were your childhood family. You often feel anxious and worried, and you try to control the situation as if it, too, were volatile. Your current perceptions are contaminated by your perceptions of the past; and your perceptions of the past have taught you to be very wary of warmth, caring, trust, freedom, choice, negotiation, give and take. It is no surprise that even in the midst of plenty, many adult children continue to starve. Or you may find that long-term intimate relationships are not possible for you. One after another, relationships become troubled and come to an end. Without a relationship, the child of an alcoholic often feels frightened and empty. However, while involved in a relationship, he or she feels mistrustful and obsessed with it. Children of alcoholics often place themselves in situations in which they feel they cannot win.

Often the adaptive behaviors children of alcoholics learn at home help them become professionally successful adults. For example, they have learned how to take responsibility, how to control, how not to be spontaneous, and to put up a front of bravado—or whatever is needed for the situation. They have learned to read people. Some of those skills can enhance their careers. Indeed, these skills may even predict their career field. But these are also the same skills that can keep them feeling unhappy inside and uncomfortable in their intimate relationships. While they have learned the hows and whens of control and responsibility, they do not know the hows and whens of letting go and surrendering.

Even though adult children of alcoholics may have married very caring persons, set up a household, and started a family, they may still find that they do not fully trust and fully share. They are still separate and empty, isolating themselves even in that situation. They might be aware of not having any real, objective reason not to trust. Yet, they get caught up in the feelings of mistrust, guilt, and anxiety that rapidly follow. If they marry someone who is an alcoholic or who comes from an alcoholic family, the problems are potentially compounded, because now we have two people living together who do not trust, do not talk, do not feel. They also do not necessarily know why they feel empty and unhappy, although they look successful to other people and seem to have a good life. Too often they begin to feel that there must be something really wrong with them, that they must be bad, sick or crazy.

21. What needs to happen in the survival stage so that adult children of alcoholics can begin their recovery from the effects of parental alcoholism?

The first thing children of alcoholics need at this stage is awareness. Becoming aware that something is not working becomes the doorway to change. Children of alcoholics need to be aware that, as a result of coming from a family in which one or more parents are alcoholic, they have certain biological and psychological vulnerabilities. Things are not quite right, and this stems from the alcoholism in their childhood families. They need to make that connection.

Such awareness may come to people when they pick up a newspaper and suddenly see an article about alcoholism or children of alcoholics. Or, they might find out about a seminar, or a workshop, or a class called

"Adult Children of Alcoholics." They might be browsing through a bookstore and pick up a book about children of alcoholics. They might read Ann Landers or some local columnist who mentions that children of alcoholics are affected by alcoholism in the family. Or they might be fortunate enough to have a friend who says, "Hey, there's a talk being given on children of alcoholics. Why don't we go?" In other words, some sort of "intervention" needs to occur. This intervention becomes a springboard for the next stage of their recovery, which we call emergent awareness.

4
Emergent Awareness

22. What is emergent awareness?

Emergent awareness refers to the stage in the recovery process when adult children of alcoholics begin to become aware of the psychological, physiological, and genetic vulnerabilities that they acquired as a result of being reared in a home where there is an alcoholic. In emergent awareness children of alcoholics recognize that there was something wrong in their childhood, and they no longer need to deny it. They become free to acknowledge their experience and its effects on them.

We have found that this kind of insight is often prompted by an intervention. By an intervention we mean any event which interrupts or breaks into a person's current awareness and provides new insight.

23. What happens as a result of an intervention?

For many people, intervention is like a sunrise. Dawn begins to flood a landscape previously shrouded in darkness. The vague sense that something is wrong with life suddenly becomes understandable. Hope emerges. Clarity seems possible. Intervention provides the light, the space, and the energy for awareness to emerge and change to begin. When children of alcoholics make the connection between their current pain and past family experiences of alcoholism, the energy once used to block out feelings and past experiences can be used more productively. They are no longer trapped in the shadows of denial.

As you begin to identify yourself as the child of an alcoholic, a process we call "coming out" occurs. This is the first major step in the recovery process. "Coming out" is a term borrowed from the gay/lesbian community. However, we use it to refer to the process by which children of alcoholics of all ages recognize and label themselves as such. They no longer maintain the shroud of secrecy and shame that is the hallmark of an alcoholic family. By coming out children of alcoholics explicitly acknowledge the vulnerabilities resulting from parental alcoholism.

Initially, coming out is a personal acknowledgment. For example, while reading this guide, you may be making connections between the written words and your personal experiences. Later, when you are ready, and there is an appropriate opportunity, it is important to share what has been learned. This "public" statement—perhaps made to a friend, perhaps expressed by attending a class for children of alcoholics—is a second and very powerful step. When this sharing is done with other adult children of alcoholics, a wonderful discovery is made—*You are not alone!*

Often the person raised by alcoholic parents thinks that his or her story is so unique, so totally different that nobody else could have experienced it. One of the things that we have noted in our classes as we describe the typical experiences of children of alcoholics is that people begin to feel as though we already know them, as though somehow we had told their personal life stories. When adult children are around other adult children and listen to their stories, their jaws drop and their eyes widen. They realize, often for the first time, that they are really not as alone, as different, as bad, as sick or as crazy as they thought. What a liberating experience! The power of this awareness is remarkable. It is this awareness that releases energy and allows the unfolding of the subsequent stages. It precipitates the end of suffering without meaning and the beginning of awareness that there really is a reason why you feel the way you do.

24. What feelings follow coming out?

We have just described the breaking down of the isolation from which children of alcoholics suffer. One of the main messages the child of an alcoholic gets at home is, "There is nothing wrong here, and don't you dare tell anyone about it!" So children of alcoholics build walls that separate them from their own experience as well as from other people. As these walls crumble in emergent awareness, there is an initial relief and excitement. Often there is also a desire to share what is happening. Then something else may begin to develop. Shortly after acknowledging that a parent is alcoholic, adult children may begin to feel bad. They begin to feel guilty. They feel as though they have betrayed the family secret and, therefore, the family itself. In reality, they have simply stopped colluding with the family on the issue of alcoholism.

Coming out, which is so profoundly essential to the recovery process, is in many ways a declaration of independence. It allows the adult child to begin an emotional separation from the family of origin and the family illness. Physical separation may have occurred through a geographic move or a death, but emotional separation inevitably comes late, comes slowly, and comes with difficulty. Frequently, a sense of violation and guilt signals this important transition.

Other feelings that can soon follow are grief and anger. An awareness grows that not only was much missing in childhood, and many of their needs were unmet, but also that they *deserved* better care. What occurs is not unlike mourning—a mourning for a lost childhood. As recovery progresses, the belief that adult children of alcoholics did deserve more will begin to infuse all aspects of their lives. At first, this is a foreign feeling. It may be upsetting and even frightening. It may cause the adult child of an alcoholic to think of himself or herself as "selfish," or "uppity.

As adult children become increasingly aware of having been cheated out of their childhood, a wave of anger is likely to ensue. The adult child may want to be forgiving, but will still feel angry. Sometimes the anger is directed not at the alcoholic, but at the sober parent—the parent who seemingly should have known better and should have protected the child. Or, anger may surface towards relatives or neighbors. As one man stated through his tears, "They saw what was happening. They knew how I was being treated. But they didn't do a thing!"

Soon all kinds of feelings begin to pour out as the adult child makes more and more connections. A rush of anxiety, sometimes bordering on terror, is not uncommon. You have probably had the experience of walking into bright sunshine after being in a darkened room. Initially, the intensity of the glare is so bright that it is painful. It takes a moment for the eyes to adjust. Gradually, things begin to clear up and become recognizable. Similarly, when you remove the lid from a pot of boiling water, pressure and steam are released. When adult children of alcoholics release their pent up feelings, the experience may be equally intense. A flood of powerful feelings can be frightening. Children of alcoholics, especially, are taught to fear such strong emotions. These early feelings, however frightening, will be useful later as a reference point from which to gauge progress. And, feelings do change—that is their nature. They will not always be so intense or overwhelming. Remind yourself also that feelings are not the same as behavior. If every thought or feeling were equal to action, we would all be in trouble.

The experience of fear or anxiety at this point is a clear signal that you are beginning to allow yourself to experience long-hidden emotions. This is absolutely necessary for recovery.

25. What are some of the pitfalls at this stage?

There are common pitfalls we see over and over. It helps to be forewarned so that when they occur, recovering adult children can negotiate them successfully. What often initially occurs is an urgency to share their new learnings with immediate family members. Many want to rush home, call up siblings or write a letter to every family member saying, "Guess what I found out?" Much to their surprise and pain, they often discover that others do not want to hear it. They may find a door slammed in their face, a cold reception, or no acknowledgment at all. As we have mentioned earlier, it is not at all uncommon for one sibling to say to the other, "What alcoholism? What are you talking about? Don't say that about our family! There's no alcoholism here. What's the matter with you?"

We suggest that you be thoughtful and move at a slow pace. Do not rush forward hoping to be the salvation of the family. When we describe the core issues adult children face, we will talk about the urge to do everything or nothing, and the need to take care of or rescue other people. This is one of the first points in the recovery process where the child of an alcoholic has the opportunity to practice a new behavior and to initially savor his or her emergent awareness as a personal gift. It will be much more rewarding to share coming out with a receptive group of friends or other children of alcoholics who are experiencing a similar awareness than to try to force changes on unwilling family members.

Another pitfall which many adult children of alcoholics experience is a tendency to attribute either all or none of life's troubles to parental alcoholism. Neither extreme is helpful. We knew one man who used his emergent awareness as an excuse for every problem he had, including polio. Another woman, still deeply caught in her own emergent guilt, could not allow herself the comfort of the adult child of alcoholic label; she would not "use *that* as an excuse." What she could not see was that while she was *not* responsible for being a child of an alcoholic, she *was* responsible for doing something about her recovery.

A related problem that children of alcoholics frequently face is lack of patience. Armed with their new found awareness, they immediately assume they should be cured. They believe they should become perfect.

They often expect to stop experiencing pain, or to stop repeating their co-alcoholic or para-alcoholic behaviors. If you find yourself at this stage, be generous with yourself. Allow yourself to continue to make mistakes; use them as opportunities to gather more information about yourself. For example, if you let someone treat you badly while you say nothing (only to seethe afterward), congratulate yourself for recognizing what happened. Give yourself permission to avoid that person in the future or plan how you would like to handle it next time. Consider it as an area where you will have lots of chances to learn.

With all the new energy and motivation, as well as the tendency to want to fix things today—if not yesterday—we again urge you to slow down, to take your time. Even in reading this book you can practice taking your time. Learning is much more powerful and lasting when it is spread out over time. You might decide that this is a good time to put the book down, to disconnect, to take a walk, or to do something different. The plans you might be making to improve yourself all at once can wait a while. Before you go on reading, take a slow, deep breath and think about how far you have come. As you go forward, remind yourself to take time out to congratulate yourself on the distance already covered.

26. What is the best way to take care of myself at this stage?

First, you need to truly accept that it is legitimate to take care of yourself. You *must* take care yourself. You are in transition, making changes, adding to your store of knowledge. Some thoughts and feelings that you have not experienced for a long time might be coming into your awareness. This is a vulnerable time. Do not deny this; you have done that long enough. Taking care of yourself might involve taking breaks, moving slowly, as well as thinking over the differences between what you feel, what you think, and how you behave. Taking care of yourself also means giving yourself permission to set new priorities. Your first priority right now can be to take care of your recovery—not the recovery of your family.

Be gentle to yourself. When you make a mistake, recognize it as a sign that you are growing. Success is getting up one more time than you fall down. Compliment yourself for starting on a new path. Give to yourself. It is time to learn. Start with small steps, scheduling activities and time with people who nourish you. Begin to surround yourself with people who can understand and who care about you. That in itself may be a new behavior. Think about who is being responsive and supportive as you go through your emerging awareness. This is really easier than it might sound. All you have to do is to just mention, for example, that you are taking a class or reading a book about adult children of alcoholics. Then simply pause and observe. Notice how the other person deals with your statement; notice how he or she responds to you. Notice, too, how *you* feel afterwards. If you feel diminished, foolish, or bad, you have learned something very valuable about your interaction with that person. You have learned that this person is not supportive of what is happening to you right now. If, on the other hand, the result of sharing some of your experiences with someone else is that you feel a bit better about yourself, a bit safer, understood and cared about, you might share a little more. Then once again stop, look, and listen. Notice how you feel. If you feel diminished, or bad, you may have reached the limit of what you can confide in this person. If, on the other hand, you still feel comfortable, you can continue to share your thoughts and feelings.

Another very important way to take care of yourself at this point is to start *listening carefully to yourself.* Listen to hear what you need or want. Many adult children of alcoholics have been systematically taught to ignore their internal messages. For example, one client we worked with described how she had been sexually molested as a small child. She had felt bad and guilty each time it happened. However, because her parents knew about it and had ignored it, she concluded that there must have been something wrong with her. After all, if there were something wrong with the abuse, surely it would have been stopped. Years later, recalling the experience, she felt confused and numb. She had never been allowed to respond to her internal messages. Now is the time to begin listening again to what is going on inside you. Begin to trust yourself again and use your feelings as a barometer of what is working for you and what is working against you. You have more resources now than you had as a child. Knowing yourself better will make a difference now; it could not have then.

27. What resources are needed?

In addition to friends who are already in your life, one of the finest resources is Al-Anon. Patterned after Alcoholics Anonymous, Al-Anon is for the friends and family of the alcoholic. Although there have always been adult children in Al-Anon, this group is becoming increasingly recognized as a resource for those whose lives have been affected by a parent's alcoholism. Registration of adult children Al-Anon Family Groups at Al-Anon's World Service Office has grown rapidly. Al-Anon is a place to learn what it has been like for other people who have been close to an alcoholic. It is a fellowship of people who share many of your concerns and experiences; it can help you understand that you are not alone. In Al-Anon you will hear how others have helped themselves as they have become more and more aware of their co-alcoholism and para-alcoholism.[30] Al-Anon can be another breath of fresh air for you.

It is important to realize that not all Al-Anon meetings are the same. If your first contact is not satisfying, we suggest that you attend at least six other meetings before you draw any conclusions. As with the process we described for evaluating the support of your friends, begin by sharing a little bit. Go to one meeting; see how you feel afterwards. Value and honor those feelings. Try again in another situation and see how that feels for you.

Another major resource at this point in your recovery could be any workshop, seminar, reading material, or class that gives you more information on adult children of alcoholics, alcoholism, co-alcoholism, or para-alcoholism. Utilize these various resources knowing that some of the information may not quite fit. Take what is useful and leave the rest.

You may want to consider counseling or psychotherapy. You may find that initially individual psychotherapy, rather than group therapy, can be very helpful. Even if you have had therapy in the past, you may be better able to use it now. In the same way that you may have found an Al-Anon group, seek a therapist who is right for you. Interview prospective therapists, preferably over the telephone. That way it may not cost you anything. It is crucial that the therapist be thoroughly familiar with the issues of alcoholism and its impact upon families. Simple questions to ask may include the following: "What is alcoholism?" "Does it affect the family?" "How does alcoholism affect the child in an alcoholic home?" "What is Al-Anon and how does it help?" and "Must I forgive my parents right now to recover?" Listen carefully to obtain the information you need. If the answers are unclear, incorrect, or leave you feeling guilty and dumb for even asking, look upon the therapist with suspicion. Not all therapists are helpful.

We particularly recommend that you seek a therapist who can be a "SOB with a heart." That encompasses two characteristics that we regard as essential ingredients in any therapeutic relationship. "SOB" refers to the therapist's willingness to confront you, to be honest with you, and not be intimidated by either you or the disease of alcoholism. "With a heart" means that the therapist will also care about how you feel and how you experience the confrontation. He or she should be able to convey both qualities to you. The therapist's responses to your questions, as well as his or her knowledge and attitudes about alcoholism, are more important than whether or not the therapist is from an alcoholic family. They are more important than whether the therapist is a psychoanalyst, or a Jungian, or a Rogerian, or a Gestaltist.

We also believe you need to become educated: it is important that you learn about alcoholism[34,37,40,52] and its effects on the family.[22,54,57] Our knowledge about alcoholism has been changing rapidly in recent years. Already, many books written in the 1960s and even in the 1970s are outdated. We suggest that you gather whatever current information is available to you. Books that we think are particularly valuable are listed in Appendix A.

However, most important is the cultivation of the attitude that you are your primary resource. For some that will sound crazy because, at this point, you may be experiencing confusion, anxiety, and panic. What you need to know is that these feelings are appropriate and are indeed indications of what you need and how you should take care of yourself right now. These feelings contain valuable information and messages; do not ignore them. As you begin to align yourself with resources outside of yourself, you can use your feelings as guides. By paying attention to what happens inside you after your interactions with an individual, you can measure that person's level of support for you at this stage of recovery. Your internal experience is your best guide.

28. How much can I count on other people to be helpful?

You should be prepared for negative comments from others. They may suggest that you are wasting time, or that you are blaming today on yesterday. For those of you in Alcoholics Anonymous, this journey can result in distance from a sponsor or from an A.A. friend with children of their own. They may not be able to support your emergent awareness. This can cause confusion and sadness as you continue on your new path. Recognize the limitations of others and be aware that your journey may also be scary to others. First and foremost, align yourself with yourself. You do possess resources within yourself. And remember, as you go forward, it is not courage if you are not afraid.

29. How do I deal with my parents at this stage (whether they are dead or alive, near or far)?

Deal with your parents cautiously, slowly, and thoughtfully if at all. Again, the primary person to take care of is you—not your parents. As we pointed out earlier, a common reaction to emergent awareness is wanting to save your parents from alcoholism and/or co-alcoholism. That is not your responsibility. This "flight into parental salvation" can be a way to avoid dealing with your own problems. Do not rush to share information or literature with your parents. If they learn about your experiences and education, do not expect them to be happy for you. Do not expect them to acknowledge what you are doing or that there is alcoholism in the family. Even if they acknowledge its presence, they might still deny its effects.

You might feel that these comments do not apply to you and that is fine. Everything we have said is true, except when it is not true! If your overriding experience tells you that you need to deal with your parents now, do so; but do it in a way that also allows you to take care of yourself. When they respond to what you tell them, use this as an opportunity to hear what they say. Understand beforehand, however, that it is not necessary for them to respond in one certain way for you to be all right; indeed, they do not have to respond at all. They can be supportive or not; they can be validating or not. Your recovery is not contingent upon your parents' approval or disapproval. Nor is it dependent on *their* recovery.

If through the normal course of events you find yourself in the company of your parents and other family members, use it as an opportunity to gather information about yourself. Watch yourself to see how you interact. Pay close attention to your feelings and your responses to other family members. This may be a good time to begin keeping a journal. This may be the time to list your different feelings. This may be a time to watch, to listen, to attend—not to judge, evaluate, or change.

30. Is it necessary to deal with the past and dredge up all that pain?

There is an old proverb which says, "The truth will make you free, but first it will make you miserable." So, yes, it really is necessary, and it really is safe to dethrone the tyranny of your past. No pain is so devastating as the pain a person refuses to face, and no suffering is so lasting as the suffering left unacknowledged.[11,12] Hidden pain becomes a tyrant determining where you can go, what you can do, and when you are comfortable. As a child, it may have been necessary to bury certain traumatizing experiences. If a child is being abused emotionally, physically, or sexually and there is no one to turn to for help, she or he might think, "It's not really that bad. It's no big deal. In fact, it doesn't even bother me that much." Such denial can allow children to live through horrors which, if fully comprehended, might be devastating. To bury the pain was to ensure survival as a child.

As an adult, however, far more resources are available, including the ability to simply get out of a situation. Adults can pack their bags and leave. Adult children of alcoholics have other people to turn to. They can find a therapist, call the police, or ask a friend for help. Adults also have more emotional resources. They now know for a fact that they can survive. To be reading this book means you made it. You have survived. You are in a position to fully learn the meaning and significance of your early experiences—how they are still affecting you today. As an adult, you can handle the challenge of facing the past and freeing yourself from its bondage. To continue to repress the pain is to continue to tell yourself that you are too helpless to deal with it. This in itself is a crippling belief. Denial of pain takes great energy and requires the person to bankrupt himself maintaining his fears.[49]

As children, many of the conclusions we draw are subverbal and implicit, based upon the realities of a child's world. When these beliefs are retained into adulthood, they continue to affect us until we have the opportunity to examine and update them in the light of the adult's reality. Until that time, we are doomed to repeat past behavior—even though it is no longer appropriate or functional.

For example, one of our clients continually went through difficult relationships with men. It was not until her third divorce that she began to realize that a pattern was repeating itself. She would fall wildly in love with a man who in turn would fall wildly in love with her. After a brief period of time they would become lovers or spouses. Some time later she would begin to notice his dependency—either on her, or on alcohol, or both. She would begin to feel overwhelmed, smothered, then resentful. There would follow a loss of respect and, ultimately, a need to get away. Seeing it happen over and over helped her realize that, somehow, she must be playing a part in these encores. As she floundered about, going from therapist to therapist, workshop to workshop, she ran across an article about adult children of alcoholics. Something connected. As she moved through the stages of recovery, she began to see the connection between her adult relationships with men and her early relationship with her father.

An alcoholic and a gambler, he would often disappear and rarely was available when she needed him. As an adult, without any conscious intent, she had devised the foolproof way to avoid being abandoned again. Unfortunately, it did not work very well. Once it was clear the man she chose was unable to function adequately on his own, she lost respect, and left him—but again felt alone and lost just like she did when she was a child.

Another major piece of information to be gained from examining childhood memories in the clearer light of an adult perspective is learning that it was the parents, *not the children*, who were responsible for the inconsistency and unpredictability in family life. The chaos in your family was not your fault. It was not because of who you were. It did not happen because you were bad, or because you were not good enough, or because there was something wrong with you. It happened because of a disease—alcoholism. It was not even a question of whether or not your parents loved you; most likely they did. But because of the sicknesses of alcoholism and co-alcoholism, that love could not be expressed in a consistent, healthy, and nurturing way. If your parents sometimes accused you of causing the problems, it was because they themselves were at a loss to understand why everything was falling apart, why they were behaving the way they were, or why they were drinking the way they were. By beginning to gradually acknowledge your early painful experiences, you will be able, perhaps for the first time, to find meaning for all those feelings. Then you can begin to comfort yourself, knowing that you were not responsible for what happened.

If you find yourself experiencing fear as you read this chapter, it may be because you really are making a decision to change. Change—even positive change—is frightening. You may worry that delving into the past will overwhelm you or that you will get stuck in the pain and not be able to move. We invent ways to hide from ourselves when we lack the courage to grieve.[49] Yet, there are safe and effective ways to go back and deal with the experiences that adult children of alcoholics have endured. They do not precipitate the profound devastation that is often feared. To the contrary, by going back and facing what happened, tremendous relief and freedom can be gained as you realize you are no longer chained to the pain of your past.

31. I don't remember much from my childhood. Is that common?

In our experience almost three out of four adult children of alcoholics report significant memory losses that extend over years of childhood. This does not mean that memories were not recorded. It means that some kind of repression has occurred. The subconscious mind will do what it needs to do to protect you, to ensure your survival. We have found that in appropriate and safe settings, adult children begin to remember more and more of what happened to them as they become freer and freer from fear and denial. In fact, you may already have begun experiencing this spontaneous access to previously lost memories as you have been reading. It would not be surprising if a number of specific instances have been recalled that you have not thought of in years. This is a natural part of the recovery process.

32. Why is it important to acknowledge the alcoholism in my family?

History teaches us that if we do not acknowledge our past, we are likely to repeat it. The shocking statistics for adult children of alcoholics are that over half of them become alcoholic. Your alcoholic parents are often themselves adult children of alcoholics. We invite you to break this generational cycle by beginning to understand it. Children of alcoholics grow up with large parts of themselves walled off in darkness, unavailable for learning or for enjoying. Until those walls are removed, life cannot be fully experienced. And until those parts of yourself and your life are acknowledged, you will not know who you truly are. Acknowledgment of your past experience is a self-validation process essential to understanding and accepting yourself. It is time that there be meaning to the suffering you have endured. The truth about growing up with alcoholism will set you free. Without it there can be no daylight to illuminate your experiences. Without that illumination there can be no coming out. Without coming out and the experience of emergent awareness, there cannot be that shock of recognition and release of energy that will enable you to deal with core issues in recovery.

You picked up this book because something has not been quite right for you. So you started an exploration. You are already a seeker, aware to some degree that it is important to begin acknowledging what has happened to you. Recognition of familial alcoholism is the first step in that process. As long as adult children deny their exposure to alcoholism, they will tend to deny other aspects of themselves and the reality around them. They will not be able to accept the wide variety of emotions, beliefs, attitudes, or differences in other people. As long as children of alcoholics deny the pain and the needs resulting from being parented by an alcoholic and co-alcoholic, they will be unable to utilize all the resources and opportunities available for taking care of themselves in the present.

It is as if there is a small, scared, and abandoned child inside who has been untended for years. He or she huddles in a corner, weeping but trying not to disturb anyone, despairing of ever being taken up and held. Acknowledging the alcoholism is to acknowledge the existence and suffering of this child. Only then can we take our own childhood self into our arms, and give ourselves the love, parenting, tenderness, and consideration that we were denied in our early years and so profoundly need today. As a passage in *An Unknown Woman* describes it, ". . .there is a little girl, kept a dwarf for 30 years by a need that has only to be said out loud to be discarded. I grew up all around it, festering around a core that I didn't know existed."[35]

Once your acknowledgment of parental alcoholism has begun, once coming out has occurred, you are free to move forward. You can begin looking at the effects your childhood experiences have had on your adult life. Perhaps for the first time painful adult experiences will begin to make sense in the light of your childhood. Here is where you can begin to identify certain issues that you have continually encountered without satisfactory resolution. We have found that there are specific, identifiable, and common problem areas that result from being raised in an alcoholic family. Recognizing these common core issues becomes the foundation for the next step in the recovery process.

5
Core Issues

33. What happens to children of alcoholics as they grow up?

Children learn what they are taught. So children of alcoholics enter adulthood coping with life in the same ways which proved to be of value to them as children. They take their childhood roles, survival strategies, and rules with them into adulthood. Later, they discover that what worked in a dysfunctional, alcoholic childhood home does not serve them well in adult life. But there is a curious thing about us human beings. We tend to do the same things over and over again even when our behavior no longer pays off. The roles and rules of childhood, which once brought a semblance of safety and sanity, now bring little of either. As with the alcoholism of the parents, the roles and rules of childhood are progressive and can encase the adult child in rigid, stereotypical behaviors.

34. In what ways do childhood roles and rules later work against adult children of alcoholics?

In adulthood, overly responsible children become overly responsible adults. They tend to be overly serious, overly self-reliant, unable to trust, unable to cooperate, and unable to relax. They find it difficult to let things be. They always need to be in control and to be in charge. These responsible adults also find that the sense of responsibility and control weighs very heavily upon them. Sometimes they shed this burden of responsibility by taking a drink. Under the influence of alcohol or other drugs, they find temporary comfort and peace. They can finally let up and let go of the pressure.

When ''adjuster'' children grow up, they become ''adjuster'' adults. Like adjuster children, they pride themselves on being flexible. Few things seem to bother them. They do, however, continue to avoid taking charge and cannot make decisions easily. They have little sense of direction, choice, or power—except, of course, when they drink. Drinking or using other drugs gives them a sense of strength. Finding solace in the bottle, they no longer feel detached. Frequently, they marry responsible adults who are only too eager to provide the direction adjusters desperately want and to assume control where adjusters feel incapable.

"Placater" children grow up taking care of others while ignoring their own needs. With the skills they have learned—to be sensitive, to be able to soothe—they become "people helpers." When we look around at the health professions, we find many adult children of alcoholics. Placaters in their childhood, they grow up to become psychologists, psychiatrists, social workers, or nurses. They find it very difficult to talk about themselves or express concern about themselves—except when they drink. Using alcohol helps them feel less constrained. It increases their self-esteem and lets them forget about the needs of others—for a while, at least.

The rules of childhood—don't talk, don't trust, don't feel—often become the laws of adulthood. Accordingly, adult children of alcoholics typically do not share their innermost feelings, not even with those closest to them. They have little faith in the value of talking, and situations involving emotion make them uncomfortable. Although they seldom fully trust anyone, they can be excessively and inappropriately loyal.[58] The injunctions of the past invade the present. Adult children of alcoholics remain bound by unspoken canons, which invisibly mandate their current behaviors. Because denial is so pervasive, they seldom look beyond the present to the roots of their difficulties.

The drinking behavior of adult children of alcoholics often becomes a shock to them and a puzzle to others. After some horrible incident, an alcoholic may say to his wife, with tears in his eyes and sincerity in his voice, "That's it! I'll never drink again." Similarly, the adult child of an alcoholic declares with honesty and great determination, "It will never happen to me! I will never drink like that." He or she really means it, too; yet may become alcoholic. The theme of "oh, poor me" becomes "oh, pour me a drink."

As they limp into adulthood, adult children of alcoholics begin to experience a loneliness and a sense that things are not right. Their internal dialogue centers around feelings of inadequacy. The thought "I'm not good enough" is frequently in their minds. They have learned to discount the input from their own senses and often do not know what is happening inside them. They have been taught that feelings can be very dangerous. They know how to disconnect from almost anything or anyone, including themselves. Life does not make much sense to them.

35. What are the main problems of adult children of alcoholics?

This is an interesting question because at first blush many adult children of alcoholics seem to have it all together. Most of them look good, dress well, appear successful, and are admired. Adept at pleasing, conforming and smiling, many seem "picture-book perfect." We have discovered, for example, that when new members come into our psychotherapy groups they think, "Oh my God, what am I doing here? I don't fit in; all these people are so together!" Part way through that first or second session, when they gather the courage to say this out loud, at least one group member says, "You looked so good, I was wondering why you came." It is a case of comparing one's insides to others' outsides—a very unfair comparison.

Adult children can appear to be so well adjusted that they do not seem to need help. After all, they are survivors. You can see why the problems faced by adult children of alcoholics may have been overlooked for so long. However, those who work with alcoholic families agree almost unanimously that there are no unaffected bystanders.[7,28,53,57] Everyone in an alcoholic family incurs some kind of physical, emotional and spiritual damage. It might be as early as the first three months of pregnancy when fetal alcohol syndrome can develop if the mother drinks too much.[17] It can be even earlier, at conception, when genetic vulnerabilities or susceptibilities to alcoholism may occur.[27,48] Indeed, statistics indicate the greatest danger to adult children of alcoholics is their own alcoholism. Fifty to sixty percent of children raised in an alcoholic family will become alcoholic themselves.[8] They are also at high risk of marrying someone who is, or will become, alcoholic or shows other addictive behaviors— and not just once, but sometimes three or four times.

According to the National Association for Children of Alcoholics, adult children of alcoholics have frequently been victims of incest, child neglect, and other forms of violence and exploitation.[44] They are prone to learning disabilities, attention deficit disorders, anxiety, attempted and completed suicides, eating disorders, and compulsive achievement. A disproportionate number of those entering the juvenile justice system, courts, prisons, and mental health facilities are children of alcoholics, and the majority of people served by employee assistance programs are adult children of alcoholics![44]

Alcoholism is an equal opportunity destroyer. Everyone in its path develops problematic patterns of behavior in their personal and social lives unless they attend to their own recovery. The tragedy is that many adult children do not recognize the source of this difficulty. They just feel the pain and suffer without meaning. They appear in physicians' offices with complaints of tension, fatigue, malaise, or other stress-related problems like migraine headaches, colitis, or ulcers.[44] They appear in counselors' offices, too, where parental alcoholism may be seen as a minor influence, when, in fact, it is the major influence. Adult children of alcoholics make up a large percentage of psychotherapists' caseloads. In their contacts with mental health professionals, adult children of alcoholics are often misdiagnosed and unrecognized because their coping style tends to be approval-seeking and socially acceptable, and they themselves do not recognize the source of their distress.[58]

36. What are the most common personal issues with which adult children of alcoholics struggle?

As we look more closely at these apparently well-functioning in-dividuals, we begin to see a constellation of recurring behavioral patterns. There are certain personal issues which seem to touch nearly all adult children of alcoholics. Certain characteristics may even be so pervasive they appear to be personality traits.

Stephanie Brown and Tim Cermak at the Stanford Alcohol Clinic were among the first to identify some of these characteristics.[14,16] Although their ground breaking work was based on adult children who were in group psychotherapy, our experience indicates that these issues extend well beyond those who seek treatment.

The first and most central issue they describe is the issue of control. Control is the one word that most characterizes the interactions of adult children of alcoholics. A major source of anxiety, conflicts over control are pervasive. Denial, suppression, and repression are used in attempts to control the outward expression as well as inner awareness of thoughts, feelings and behaviors. The fear of being "out of control" is almost univer-sal, and strong feelings are experienced as being out of control. Sometimes called "hypervigilant," adult children of alcoholics automatically scan the environment for cues, wanting to know what is in front, behind, to the left and to the right of them at all times.

The second issue Brown and Cermak identify is trust or, more precise-ly, distrust—a distrust of others as well as of self. It is not difficult to under-stand how this distrust arises. Repeatedly told to ignore the obvious, children of alcoholics learn to distrust the wisdom of their own organism, to distrust what their own senses tell them. Father is asleep on the garage floor in his three-piece suit, or mother's head falls into a plate of spaghetti, and everyone who is important is saying "nothing is wrong." This leaves the children misinformed, puzzled, and bewildered! Their stomachs may hurt, their hearts may race, and the people on whom they are most dependent for survival are saying, "Don't worry, no big deal, everything is all right."

This leads to a third issue Brown and Cermak describe: the avoidance of feelings and the fundamental belief that feelings are wrong, bad, and scary. In the alcoholic family the child's expression of feelings is typically met with censure, disapproval, anger, and rejection. Often the child is told explicitly, "Don't you dare say that to me; don't even think it!" or "Don't upset your mother. You have to be more understanding." In other words, children of alcoholics are taught very early that it is necessary to hide their feelings. They soon learn not to even have any feelings. They learn to repress, deny, or minimize them. What good are they? They just cause trouble.

As if that is not enough, children of alcoholics also see how feelings can lead directly to action. When a parent is drunk, they see feelings that are unchecked because the first effect of alcohol is disinhibition and a loss of judgment. Imagine children at five, six, or even ten, living in a situation where they have an alcoholic parent, perhaps their father. Father comes home drunk and angry. Before they know it, things are being thrown, people are being hit. Anger is translated into immediate, destructive actions. In this way, feelings become associated with actions. The very notion, the very idea of having a strong feeling is equated with acting out that feeling. Instead of looking at feelings as a *potential* impetus to behavior, children of alcoholics see feelings as a direct immediate *cause* of behavior. In the midst of all this chaos and confusion, they may want to run to their parents, throw their arms around them and weep, but they know that it would not be safe. They cannot even talk about what happened! They know that in order to live in this family—and a five or even ten-year-old cannot say, "To heck with this! I'm going to pack my bags and find another family to live with,"—they *must* ignore their feelings. Shock, anger, terror, or guilt are so scary, so dangerous, so unacceptable, that the best way to deal with them is just not to acknowledge them. Instead, they must be buried deep inside.

Compounding all this is the self-centeredness of young children. They see themselves as the center of the universe. Imagine what would happen if a parent is drunk and abusive and the child wishes that something would happen to him or her. Then, for some reason, something *does* happen. With their magical thinking, children automatically and unconsciously assume their thoughts and feelings are so powerful they must have caused that to happen. A child might lie in bed at night hearing the screams or arguing of his parents and think to himself, "I wish Daddy would go away; I wish he would die." When eventually the alcoholic parent has an accident, goes to the hospital, or moves out, the child readily concludes, "It is my fault; I wished it!" All of this is "forgotten" by the adult child. Thinking back, he or she does not remember that this was somewhere at the beginning of his extreme difficulty with feelings and guilt.

It is also the beginning of another issue that Brown and Cermak describe—namely, over-responsibility. Children come to believe they are responsible for what is happening in the family. After all, it is not uncommon for parents to say, "If you hadn't talked back like that, or if you hadn't got in trouble at school today, then I wouldn't need a drink tonight." This just feeds that normal capacity for self-centeredness. Even in the absence of physical or sexual abuse, and even when childhood is not overtly traumatic, the child may still desperately and continuously feel responsible and try to remove the necessity for the parent's drinking by being a model child. He may be at the beck and call of the parents, serving as the family counselor at the age of five or as the family chauffeur at the age of twenty-five. Quite a load for anybody to bear, particularly a child. Children do not know that the alcoholic drinks because he or she has lost the choice to drink. Alcoholics do not drink because they have problems. If that were true, we would all be alcoholics. Alcoholics drink because they cannot stop.[37,40]

Because of these childhood experiences, adult children of alcoholics grow up believing they are responsible for other's emotions and actions. We frequently see this, especially in group therapy. If someone is angry, other members of the group immediately assume it is because of something they did. Similarly, if a group member is absent, others believe it is because of something they said.

The last issue that Brown and Cermak talk about is the tendency of adult children to ignore their own needs. It is easy to see how that would happen to children raised in a family in which their needs are typically secondary to alcoholism. The family disease gets first billing. It has to be checked out before anything else in the family gets taken care of. The children continually wonder: "Is daddy drunk? If daddy's drunk, then I'd better not tell him what happened today.'' ''Is mommy drinking again? If she's drinking, I'd better not tell her about the parent/teacher conference tonight, because she'll just get mad.'' One particularly aware adult child with whom we worked expressed it this way: ''My feelings were not important. When a kid on the street said something mean to me and I felt lousy, all I really wanted was to crawl up on my mom's lap, put my head on her shoulder, and ask her to hold me for a while. But if mom was sitting at the dining room table with a drink in her hand, I knew I'd better find another way to be consoled. She couldn't hold a drink in one hand and me in the other. I felt so bad, so disappointed, that I decided I didn't really need to be held at all. When I came to believe that I couldn't trust anybody to be there to hold me, I decided I wouldn't *let* anybody hold me!''

Adult children may find that acknowledging their personal needs leads them to feel guilty, because they have learned to regard their needs as an imposition on others. They also frequently have a sense that if they ask for something, the other person now knows something dangerously important about them. To have needs is to be vulnerable and in the past it certainly did not pay to be vulnerable. If they do not feel guilty or vulnerable, they may feel dependent, less capable, or obligated to the person who met their needs. These are all emotions contrary to feeling in control. Therefore, personal needs had best be avoided, ignored, or denied.

37. What other personal issues might result?

In addition to the five central issues that Brown and Cermak identified, we have seen other issues which recur so frequently that we regard them also as core issues for adult children of alcoholics. We have observed these issues in adult children who are in psychotherapy as well as with those who have come to public lectures, classes, and workshops. The most prominent of these issues is what we refer to as ''all-or-none functioning'': that is, the tendency to think, feel, and behave in an all-or-none way. Everything is black or white—there is no in-between. Things are either all right or all wrong, and since things are seldom all right, they are often all wrong.

Like the need to have control, all-or-none functioning pervades other issues. For example, adult children of alcoholics approach the issue of trust from an all-or-none perspective. Lacking an appropriate role model for intimacy in childhood, they have difficulty establishing or maintaining personal relationships as adults. Bouncing back and forth between extremes, they will either trust a person totally and tell their entire history, or they will distrust so fully that they will not share anything personal. Neither strategy is effective.

All-or-none functioning colors the way adult children deal with feelings. As we have already mentioned, adult children of alcoholics tend to associate feelings with behavior and are, therefore, reluctant to deal with emotions. If anger is expressed, for example, they are struck by fear or panic, convinced that violence may follow, or that a relationship will be severed. In their past, this may have been true.

The all-or-none approach can also result in adult children's difficulties in establishing adequate and useful boundaries between themselves and others. This is particularly true in regard to their parents, where they confuse love with need or caretaking. They frequently confuse other feelings, including intimacy with smothering, spontaneity with irrationality, and relaxation with depression. This confusion of feeling states further contributes to their difficulties with personal boundaries and relationships. The inability to function in terms of degree invariably predisposes adult children of alcoholics to failure. Because of the all-or-none approach, they are not able to utilize information from their environment very well as experiences are forced to fit their black and white view of the world. This all-or-none characteristic also obstructs adult children's ability to take things one step at a time, to break down a task into smaller and therefore more manageable steps or pieces.

Like control, all-or-none functioning is a direct outgrowth of childhood experiences. We often see this extreme black-or-white functioning in alcoholic families. Many alcoholics, guilty after a drunken episode, accept outrageous behavior from those they feel they have wronged. Then, when drunk again, they may release the resentment that has built up, expressing anger at everything and everyone. There may be a repeated series of interactions with a parent who, for example, one day sits you on his lap, pats you on the head, and with the smell of whiskey on his breath says, "You're so wonderful. You're the perfect child. You make my life so happy that I don't know what I would do without you." The next day that parent has a hangover and is feeling irritable. You come home from school, the door bangs, and suddenly you have someone screaming at you, saying that you are a horrible child, that you are the cause of all his problems, and that you never do anything right! In other words you are all right or you are all wrong; there is no in-between, only extremes. That is life in an alcoholic home.

Another issue we have observed consistently is dissociation. Dissociation is the separation or split in the wholeness of an experience—not unlike an emotional anesthesia. An example is a person who describes a scene of great pain from her childhood, crying as she talks; yet, when asked what she is feeling, she will honestly reply, "Nothing." Asked why she is weeping, she will answer, "I don't know." She does not connect the tears, the memory, and the emotion. It is as though a car started forward as expected, but once moving down the street, the clutch was disengaged and it continued in neutral. The outward manifestation of dissociation can be described as "flattened affect," and functions as self-protection.[30] Dissociation causes many adult children of alcoholics to look "spaced out" or "tranced out." It is as though they are in some kind of fog.

Many adult children of alcoholics describe absolutely horrifying situations or events as though they were normal, everyday affairs. When attention is called to the outrageous quality of the events, there is often a wide-eyed surprised response, "Oh, is that unusual? It happened all the time at our house!" For instance, a client recently described how he would stand nearby and listen while his folks were fighting—not to eavesdrop, but to call the police or ambulance when it was needed. He went on to say his brother had killed himself and now his sister was physically abusing their mother. All this was said in a calm voice with a slight smile. Whatever his feelings might be, he had separated himself from them, as if the story he was telling had no personal impact.

Another issue we have encountered is the tendency for children raised in the chaotic environment of an alcoholic family to become "adrenalin junkies." Accustomed to frequent crises and emergencies, adult children of alcoholics may find themselves depressed or anxious when life is stable and uneventful. It might take years before they recognize that every time life is calm and relationships with others seem good, they feel uncomfortable. At this point they often stir things up. With no other goal in life than to survive from crisis to crisis, to go without a crisis is to go into withdrawal. It takes another emergency, another adrenalin rush, for them to feel alive and engaged. As a result, little energy is left over to build for the future when most of it is spent coping with daily crises.

These issues lead to adult children's extremely low self-esteem. Their low self-esteem comes from not trusting themselves, from not knowing their own feelings. It comes from having an all-or-none way of looking at things, so they can rarely give themselves credit for what they have accomplished unless it is perfect. It comes from a childhood in which their needs were subjugated, minimized, or ignored. And it comes from living in a world of broken promises and the belief that they were somehow responsible for the problems in their family. Since adult children of alcoholics have a difficult time seeing themselves as valuable or worthwhile, they have a difficult time realizing their right to be treated well, to set limits on what they will and will not do, or what they will and will not tolerate. All of this adds up to an adult who lacks a sense of personal rights.

38. In what situations are these issues most noticeable?

We have observed that there are certain types of situations, certain events, which consistently trigger the core issues we have been describing. By far the most frequent are those situations requiring trust, warmth, sharing, spontaneity, flexibility—in short, intimate relationships. This may be the one area where the child of an alcoholic knows something is wrong. This is often the area that brings adult children into therapy or leads them to seek help. They begin to see that over and over in their intimate relationships they run into conflicting feelings or behavior patterns that do not work. Maybe they have just been through their fourth painful relationship and finally suspect a pattern. They repeatedly align themselves with people who are unavailable or unsupportive, people who are alcoholic or addicted to other drugs, or people who are very dependent and needy. Because of the immediate distress in their intimate relationships, they frequently do not bother to mention to a therapist that there is alcoholism in the family. Even if they do, too often the therapist says, "Tell me something else about your mother or father," and discounts the impact of alcoholism. The adult child may not even be aware of or able to talk about the alcoholism. As incredible as it may seem, up to 40% of adult children of alcoholics leave home without acknowledging that their parents are alcoholic. By now it should be clear why intimate relationships—which require give and take, surrender of control, an ability to see oneself as human, as changeable, as fallible, and to accept another person with similar qualities—are difficult for children of alcoholics.

Other events that act as catalysts to trigger core issues are major transitions in life. These are major life passages in which a person is undergoing significant changes and encountering new situations which require a reorganization of patterns from the past. Major life transitions include changing jobs, moving, birth of a child, a death in the family, getting married, getting divorced, entering adulthood or middle age, starting college, or graduating. All require accommodation to a new environment. The rigidity inherent in the characteristics that unrecovering children of alcoholics bring into their adult years makes smooth transitions difficult. Instead, adult children of alcoholics are often resistant to change and get "stuck" in old patterns, forgetting that even ink pens have erasers on them these days!

Yet another kind of trigger is any unexpected event. With no time to anticipate a situation or prepare a response, adult children of alcoholics will automatically fall back into their old, habitual behavior patterns— patterns which helped them survive as children but now interfere with their happiness as adults. They get anxious, shut down, enter a flurry of activity, or deny what is happening. Similarly, a visit with their family will often reactivate old responses.

Situations related to a person's performance will also act as a trigger. When there is a standard or a performance level to be met, children of alcoholics worry about their ability to meet that standard. They re-experience their anxiety, their all-or-nothing thinking ("I'm a failure"), the sense of inadequacy, their guilt, and their lack of self-esteem. Even if the situation involves a number of people, they might assume full responsibility. They believe, "Things aren't going right at work. It's my fault." If there is an important deadline ahead, they will tell themselves they are not organized enough even though their performance might be excellent. If everything is not in perfect order, they must be doing something wrong. Indeed, the anxiety to perform perfectly may outweigh the importance of the task. Even trivial tasks may be taken to represent a global statement on their competence.

These events that commonly occur in a person's life will frequently activate the problematic core issues of adult children of alcoholics. It is clearly understandable that they cause difficulty in light of the early training received in the alcoholic family.

39. Why do I dread holidays?

As holidays approach, adult children of alcoholics tend to have mounting feelings of anxiety, depression, and confusion. Often, they do not know why. It is only after they sit down and sort through what holidays were like when they were kids that they realize more and more clearly the kinds of negative experiences that Thanksgiving, Christmas or New Year's Eve brought. For many alcoholic families, the holidays provide an opportunity for an extended binge. Alcoholics have more social permission as well as time to drink, and drink, and drink. As they continue to drink, losing more and more control, they become increasingly abusive and difficult to be around. Therefore, the child often sees the entire family going into crisis during holidays. Family fights occur at a much higher frequency; parents are less able to cope; other alcoholic relatives may visit; and more demands are made. This atmosphere is scary at best and physically dangerous at worst. Adding insult to injury, the child starts feeling responsible and begins to think, "If only I did so and so, then mom and dad wouldn't drink or fight so much or be so unhappy." Feelings of guilt are reactivated during the holidays. It is really no surprise that with the "joyous season" of the holidays approaching, adult children of alcoholics begin to feel joyless.

Children of alcoholics are likely to compare what is going on in their home during the holidays with the experience of other families. Their friends are talking about exciting, happy, and wonderful times. Other families seem to be getting along so well. Their all-or-none thinking convinces them that everybody is happy but them. This heightens their sense of loss, separation, isolation, and difference. There are also countless messages telling adult children how great everything is supposed to be on this wonderful holiday. Television commercials and advertisements proclaim the festivity of the occasion. No wonder so many adult children of alcoholics feel crazy on holidays! They experience two opposing messages. Their own nervous system is telling them they hurt, while everyone else is telling them it is a happy time. It is just like when they were kids—their parents were telling them nothing was wrong but they felt as if everything was wrong.

The prospect of spending time with their parents during holidays puts children of alcoholics in a no-win position. If they decide to spend the holiday with the family, they are implicitly saying, "All right, I'm going to put up with all this crazy, out-of-control, drunken behavior." If, on the other hand, they say, "No, I'm not going to do this. I'm not going to go home and spend the holidays with my family" they feel guilty. They feel like a bad child again. A "good" child, of course, would go home and suffer through all of the required indignities for the sake of the family. And, sometimes drinking is the admission ticket to the family; the only way to be with the family is to drink.

Unrecovering adult children of alcoholics rarely recognize all these influences. They are pushed and pulled emotionally without identifying the source of the pressure. Besides, feelings are not acceptable, and they cannot talk about what is happening. Again they suffer without meaning. For them, a holiday is often experienced as a *holidaze*!

40. What is the best way to take care of myself while I am confronting core issues?

The answer to this question is similar to how adult children would take care of themselves in any of the preceding or subsequent stages. But it is especially important in the stage of core issues to realize and to really appreciate that this is a very special period of time. Once adult children of alcoholics acknowledge and accept the influence of the past, they are ready to deal with the core issues which have plagued them as adults. If the familial alcoholism is ignored or minimized, they will progress very slowly or not at all. That is why many adult children who are in psychotherapy and do not deal with their parents' alcoholism seem to flounder and get nowhere. Without a foundation, not much of a building can be erected. Without knowing about alcoholism, without knowing how alcoholism affects the family and everyone in it, there is no context in which to understand what has happened.

Acquiring certain new attitudes toward yourself and toward others is crucial in this stage; they pave the way for the changes that need to occur. First and foremost, cultivate the attitude that it is better to explore than to criticize. Be grateful when you discover a problem area. After all, it was there all the time! Be open to new ways of seeing things, to new meanings, new learnings, new associations, without being judgmental. Make few conclusions about yourself or others until you have had a chance to gather a lot of information. Know how deep the water is before you jump in. Here again, it is important to slow down, take your time, and develop patience. Remember, it took years to get to where you are now; you cannot fix everything in a day.

While developing these attitudes, you may want to enlist the aid of a guide or consultant. One of the things adult children of alcoholics desperately need to learn is to reach out and ask for help. At this stage, give yourself permission to say, "I think I need some assistance." You may want to seek a therapist if you have not done so already. All the things that we have said about choosing a therapist apply at this stage. And, you would certainly want to continue your education on alcoholism. If you have not yet gone to an Al-Anon meeting, this would be the time to start attending. See what this support group has to offer you. Since all Al-Anon meetings are different, try attending several. Many communities have special meetings for adult children of alcoholics. You have nothing to lose and everything to gain.

If you find that you are isolated from others, let that be a sign—like a red flag—which indicates you are in trouble. There are other red flags during this stage that suggest this is the right time to get help: 1) feeling overwhelmed with what you are learning, experiencing, or seeing; 2) not having the foggiest idea about what to do next; 3) not having any friends or family to talk to; 4) excessive criticism of yourself or others; 5) strong feelings of depression and anxiety or insecurity and fear; 6) frequent bouts of insomnia and 7) the big one, namely excessive alcohol or other drug consumption. If you are not sure what kind of help you need, contact someone you trust to get some feedback that will help you assess whether you need help, and, if so, how to get it.

41. What are the pitfalls at this stage?

We have pointed out in the previous question that there is a possibility that you will not take care of yourself, or that you may not acknowledge needing to take care of yourself. Even knowing all that you know now, you might still believe that *you* were not affected by the alcoholism in your family. After all, your parents did not sexually or physically abuse you. So, a major pitfall is continuing to minimize the impact of parental alcoholism. You might tell yourself that your childhood was not really all that stressful or traumatic. Perhaps you might experience a flight into activity, thinking now is the time to fix everything, including the alcoholic, the co-alcoholic, and all of the other family members. You may plunge into educating all your friends with missionary zeal, watching the ones who drink, evaluating their drinking, and diagnosing alcoholism. All this does is direct your attention away from your own difficulties. On the other hand, you might be so overwhelmed by all of the new things that you are learning that you will just want to chuck it and say, "It's too much; there is no way I can make my life better." A feeling of hopelessness may take over for a while. That is a major pitfall.

Another pitfall is to again confuse your feelings with your behavior. For example, while you might feel overwhelmed, you are probably still getting out of bed in the morning. You still get dressed, comb your hair, brush your teeth. You still go to work and get chores done around the house. In other words, you still continue to function, although it might be a lot harder. This is not unusual! When you begin confronting core issues, regular daily tasks can become more of a chore. You have less energy for them because you are spending more energy on understanding, learning, and dealing with yourself as the adult child of an alcoholic. You might berate yourself for not being healed, not being recovered, not being totally all together right away. "After all," you might say to yourself, "now I know the issues. I should do better. I don't have any excuses." You can avoid this pitfall if you are more kind to yourself and more understanding.

Perhaps the greatest pitfall of all for adult children of alcoholics is underestimating the pervasive, insidious effects of alcoholism and the depth of the core issues they face. One result is an unrealistic expectation of a speedy recovery. Then, if you are having a hard time, you may blame yourself and feel that you have totally failed to "cure" yourself. Watch out for this all-or-none tendency. It may appear as all-or-none thinking, all-or-none feeling, or all-or-none behaving. It can be very, very subtle and still devastating. When you have an all-or-none attitude toward your recovery, you are not being fair to yourself. It takes a long time to heal deep wounds. These are not easy issues to deal with. It has been suggested that three to five years of active participation in Al-Anon and other treatment are needed for an alcoholic family to recover.[56]

Keep in mind, too, that taking time out from the learning process is *not* a pitfall. This can be life-enhancing in a positive way and a sign of your own good judgment about what is right for you. For example, if you find that you keep wanting to take a break from this book or from thinking about the issues raised, do so! Recovery moves at your pace; you do not move at recovery's pace.

42. How do I deal with my parents in this stage?

Repetition is an essential part of learning for all of us. So, we want to emphasize here, as we did in the last chapter, that you do not *need* to deal directly with your parents or their drinking. You do not have to educate them, fix them, or confront them. You have more than enough to do just dealing with yourself. When you have a strong impulse to deal with your parents, it is important for your own recovery to ask yourself the following kinds of questions: Why am I so preoccupied with them now? Who am I really trying to help here? What am I really trying to do? It is a mistake to think that if you first "fix" your parents, then your problems will be solved. That is not the path to recovery. Your recovery does not depend on your parents' recovery! They do not even have to acknowledge their alcoholism or co-alcoholism. It is not necessary for your growth that they know what you are learning, that they approve of what you are doing, or even that they care.

If your parent or parents are dead, it is still important to sort through the messages that you received from them and the feelings that you have about them. That is best done with professional help. There are sophisticated and powerful therapeutic methods which can enable you to finish some of your old business with them even if they are dead.

If your parents live nearby or you still live with them, you will probably find increased discomfort as you proceed through your learning and recovery. This is a positive sign. It means you are changing. Seek a support group like Al-Anon. You may not be able to deal successfully with your alcoholic parent or parents alone. It can be very painful, for example, to stop enabling your parents' drinking because in doing so it may feel cold or uncaring. Just to understand the term "enabling" is going to take time. That is why it is so important that the people helping you really know alcoholism. If you feel that your parent's life is in imminent danger and it is essential he or she gets help immediately, an intervention might be useful. An intervention is a loving confrontation of several people close to the alcoholic.[33] To explore this, contact an alcoholism therapist, agency, or hospital chemical dependency unit. They will help you get the education you need and help facilitate your own recovery as you prepare the intervention. Always remember that the first person you need to give priority, time, attention, and love to during recovery is yourself.

43. These issues seem to apply to a lot of people. Are they really unique to adult children of alcoholics?

It is certainly true that these issues apply to other people as well. They apply particularly to people who have been reared in a troubled or dysfunctional family. You may remember that Virginia Satir, a prominent figure in family therapy, identified general role behaviors that family members adopt when they are under stress.[5] Family members work very hard at these roles to save the family system even at the expense of their own emotional and physical well-being. Satir identified four main roles: the placater, who agrees with everyone and feels no self worth; the blamer, who disagrees with everyone and feels lonely and unsuccessful; the super-reasonable one, who is calm and logical but feels vulnerable; and the distractor, who makes no sense and feels nobody cares.

While not every family in stress is alcoholic, every alcoholic family is in stress.[53] We find that the issues described in this chapter, while not specific to adult children of alcoholics, are particularly marked and prevalent among them. Thus, if someone is an unrecovering adult child, we know that he or she probably has significant problems with control, all-or-none functioning, trust, poor self-esteem, and so on. There is a rigidity, an inflexibility, an inability to move out of these patterns of behavior that is characteristic of adult children of alcoholics. This is primarily because of denial. While many troubled families engage in it, denial is the hallmark of an alcoholic family. This means there is little or no chance to talk about what is happening. When there is denial of a problem like alcoholism, there is no opportunity to deal with its effects, because those too must be denied or attributed to something else.

44. What about the culturally different or the ethnic minority adult child of an alcoholic?

As we noted earlier, professionals in the alcoholism field have only recently focused their attention on children of alcoholics. Focus on the adult child is even more recent. So, while little research exists describing adult children of alcoholics in general, even less research exists identifying the issues and problems of minority adult children of alcoholics. There is even relatively little information on alcoholism in different cultures, although we believe that culture has a significant impact. The functions that alcohol serve are different in different cultures.[43] Different cultural groups do not regard alcoholism in the same way, and members of the family and cultural community play different roles in the treatment and prevention of alcoholism. In general, the greater the degree of assimilation into the Anglo culture, the more likely the messages of this book apply to the minority adult child of an alcoholic. To understand the particular issues concerning alcohol-related problems that affect members of minority groups, it is necessary to look at the political, social, and economic values of the various groups and to see how these forces influence the thoughts, feelings, and behaviors of members. Much more research has to be done before statements can be made regarding the specific roles that minority children of alcoholics adopt and the core issues they encounter as adults. In the meantime, we encourage efforts to identify the kinds of issues that ethnic minorities face in response to familial alcoholism.

Among native Americans, for example, alcoholism is a major health problem. A recent National Council on Alcoholism position paper states that 80 percent of native American college students and 50 percent of high school students drop out because of family alcoholism.[42] Children in alcoholic native American families hear conflicting messages about alcohol use. They see that the excessive drinking by male family members is acceptable. Although there are almost 500 different tribes recognized by the federal government, each with its unique cultural patterns, many native Americans regard alcoholism as a disorder of the spirit, not a physical disorder.[43] It is often seen as punishment for wrongdoing by supernatural forces. This view makes alcoholism difficult to identify as a disease and to treat effectively.

Among the Hispanic populations of this country (the word Hispanic is used in reference to persons of Spanish-speaking origin, including Mexican, Mexican-American, Cuban, Puerto Rican, Central and South American), it is possible to note several general characteristics relevant to the use and abuse of alcohol. Because of the traditional respect in Hispanic families for elders, it is difficult to break the shroud of secrecy and denial. The stage of emergent awareness will be especially difficult as these adult children begin to acknowledge the reality of their childhood, make public an issue generally considered to be a moral question belonging within the family, and experience the "betrayal" of their family. Making personal problems public is tantamount to bringing disrespect upon the family. There is usually less opportunity for, or acceptance of, children confronting their parents. As one Mexican man emphatically stated, "It's none of my business if my mother gets drunk! She's had a hard life. She's worked all this time and raised all us kids. If she wants to drink in her last years—let her!" Alcoholism is often not identified until the late stages of the disease because heavy drinking is often tolerated until economic responsibilities can no longer be met.[21]

Moral weakness is generally seen as the origin of alcoholism in the black community.[43] The belief that alcoholism is a moral issue rather than a disease has prevented many black families from seeking professional help. When drinking has interfered with family responsibilities, other members have turned to their extended families and community networks of churches and social clubs for assistance rather than to professional mental health agencies.

Minority adult children of alcoholics need to be particularly sensitive to their own needs, and extremely conscientious in building a group of supportive friends during the recovery process. With this in mind, the minority adult child can make use of what does fit for him or her from this book and other related literature. "After all," as one minority colleague stated, "pain is pain." Many of the basics will be the same.

45. How will I ever be able to get rid of all these problems?

We get some of our most startled looks when we state that virtually every apparent liability that adult children of alcoholics have can also be regarded as an asset in the right context. For instance, there are many situations in which control and responsibility are wonderful assets. We would want the proofreader of our book to be an adult child of an alcoholic.

We are reminded of a woman in one of our psychotherapy groups. She had an old car. We mean a *really* old car! It sat in front of her house day in and day out because it no longer worked. Not only did it not run, but it was an eyesore. The paint had faded, it had dents, a flat tire, and was covered with dirt. Oil leaked out the bottom onto the ground below. The grass underneath was dying. The neighbors began to feel irritated whenever they saw that old, beat-up car. They wanted her to change things. She insisted that it was hopeless. One weekend, a classic car show came through town. Shortly after, the neighbors began to notice that the woman was working on her car. She had started taking a class on auto restoration and was reading several books on the subject. Before long, she had the engine running. She hired some experts to work on the transmission because she was not able to repair it herself. Much to her surprise and relief, it was not damaged nearly as badly as she thought—even after all that misuse. She just spent an hour or two each and every day working on the repair project, took things one at a time, and kept at it. She started to treat that car as if it needed care just like a person. She got around to restoring the parts that had broken down. She painted it a beautiful bright color and bought new tires. Eventually she created a valuable vintage automobile from a previously embarrassing car that did not function.

We would like to suggest that you begin to look at yourself in some new ways. Do not be too quick to throw out all those "negative" characteristics. Instead, keep them and transform them. See how they can be valuable in your current life. With loving attention from you and a little help from others, you can begin to make changes, step by step. Confronting core issues, with new insights into the nature of your problems, you will also discover new strengths. In fact, you can even begin to enjoy the process of change.

6
Transformations

46. What is a transformation and how does the transformations stage fit into the recovery process?

A transformation is a change. It might be as simple as experimenting with one new behavior or it might involve a more complex alteration in personality or character. Personal growth is always a process of change, of transformation. For adult children of alcoholics, the journey to recovery will take them through many transformations. They will take the characteristics they developed to survive as children and discover how to use them to better suit the circumstances of their adult life. New ways of looking at old behaviors can be learned.

To foster the transformations stage of recovery is to make it a priority. Give it your time. Give it your attention. Give it your energy. Seek opportunities to put into effect some of the things you are learning. Dare to talk about what is happening to you. Dare to trust at least one person. Dare to feel your emotions. See what happens when you break the injunctions of the past. Above all, be patient with yourself. Patience could be the hardest task of all. This chapter will describe a number of further steps which you can take. Through transformations you start becoming part of the solution and not part of the problem.

And remember, you do not *have to* change! What you decide to do, or not to do, is up to you. You can live with things as they are, but is this what you really want?

47. How can I begin to work through what happened to me?

You have already begun. Reading this book is one step you have already taken. This step, in itself, is an accomplishment we encourage you to acknowledge and to feel good about. Recognition makes it real.

There is an old proverb which says, "The beginning of wisdom is to call things by their right name." Calling things by their right name helps bring about transformations. When core issues are recognized and identified by adult children of alcoholics, more and more of their behaviors can be seen in the context necessary to change them. Core issues provide a new vocabulary, a new way to describe and understand current behaviors. Armed with the skill of acknowledgment, a tool for transformations, adult children of alcoholics have a way to label their own eternal yesterdays— the todays shaped and fashioned by the past. Armed with this historical perspective, meanings can be found and connections made between the present and the past. Only then can choice become possible and freedom be discovered.

For years, core issues have been a dark umbrella under which repetitive, problematic behaviors occurred. Now there is the chance to utilize these very issues to move forward to a life of meaning and joy. By respecting your genetic, physiological, and psychological vulnerabilities and by watching your own attitudes, you place yourself in a position to derive the benefits of being someone who could survive in spite of unpredictability, inconsistency, arbitrariness, and chaos. Not everyone does. Not everyone knows how to make lemonade when life gives them a lemon. So sit back and explicitly acknowledge to yourself, and someone else too, just how far you have come. You can begin to look forward to enjoying life—not just surviving it. You, indeed, are on your way to recovery!

48. Why are issues of control and all-or-none functioning so central to adult children of alcoholics?

When we look at the various personal issues adult children of alcoholics face, we find the need to control coupled with a difficulty in seeing life's shades of gray woven throughout the fabric of their thoughts, feelings, and behaviors. Control and all-or-none functioning are crucial to understanding how adult children organize their lives. They are at the heart of all those repetitive, self-defeating patterns of behavior which typically characterize adult children of alcoholics. These two issues manifest themselves in many subtle ways. They frequently can be disguised as perfectionism, hypervigilance, and unrelenting motivation. They masquerade as anxiety, depression, and guilt. When these behaviors are in full force, it is difficult for recovery to proceed.

When we use the word control, we are talking about the compulsive need to be in charge of everything and everyone. It is much more than a selfish desire to have things one's own way. It is a compulsion to keep tight reins on the expression and awareness of thoughts, feelings, and behaviors. It is manifested in adult children of alcoholics' need to direct, lead, instruct, supervise, regulate, or legislate their own and others' behavior. The need to control is seen in their discomfort with surprises, with criticism, with not knowing what will happen next, or with strong feelings. Having gone through childhood with little or no control, it is as if adult children have silently vowed, "Never again." As they enter adulthood, the need to control what happens becomes paramount.

During childhood the need for control was critically important. Children need to believe they can exercise some influence over what goes on around them. It is too frightening for them to consider that nothing they can do will make a difference. They really need to convince themselves that if only they did or were such and such, then their parents would stop drinking or fighting, and everything would be fine. So they began playng the "if only" game very early in an attempt to adapt the world, their world, to their own safety and security needs.

When we discussed Brown and Cermak's work, we described the five issues they identified—namely, control, trust, personal needs, feelings, and overresponsibility.[14, 16] They consider control so pervasive that it affects the other four issues. For example, to trust someone is to give up some control, and this is felt to be dangerous, because it gives others control over you. We have heard adult children of alcoholics say, "If I trust you, I will have to let down my guard, and then you can hurt me." To admit personal needs is seen as an admission of a loss of power, a loss of control. Many adult children say, "If others know I need something, I can't depend on their giving it to me. It's safer not to have needs; then they won't have the power to hurt me." As children, controlling feelings was necessary for survival. Emotions were like volcanoes which could erupt both in the child and others. The need to control is based on the fear that if feelings go too far, if they are not checked, another eruption will occur. That is scary. Furthermore, feeling in charge of and in control of all that happens leads to an overdeveloped sense of responsibility. If someone is sad, for example, the adult child feels responsible and will attempt to control or change the person. On the other hand, recovering adult children of alcoholics look for opportunities to let go of control.

All-or-none functioning can be even more ensnaring than control. The lack of a middle ground or a "gray scale," as one of our clients referred to it, is pervasive and insidious. For example, even after reading this book, adult children of alcoholics might believe that since they are still making mistakes and still succumbing to the core issues we have been discussing, they have failed—again. If they have not achieved full recovery by this point, they feel they have not achieved anything. If everything is not all right (which it never is), everything is all wrong! Thinking this way is falling into the trap of all-or-none functioning.

All-or-none functioning strongly influences the issue of control. Control is seen as either present (I am in control), or absent (I am out of control). I am either on top of everything or on top of nothing. Over and over, adult children of alcoholics admonish themselves not to lose control. Control is guarded like a house of cards—if one piece is moved, the whole structure might collapse. This leads to rigidity. All-or-none thinking thus magnifies potential threats to control, like the occurrence of strong feelings. Strong feelings, negative or positive, seem to verge on loss of control. If one feels anger, violence will follow. It is catastrophic thinking— if this happens, something terrible will follow! In their childhood this may in fact have occurred.

All-or-none responding also affects the issue of trust. The adult child may trust somebody so totally that, for example, on a first date, he or she will sit down and tell that person his or her whole life story—without first considering the other person's level of interest, caring, or gentleness. When this happens, the other person is likely to be overwhelmed by the onslaught of openness and will often "bow out," either gracefully or ungracefully, of the situation. The adult child then looks around, somewhat perplexed and confused, not understanding what happened. As a result, on the next date with somebody else, she or he will not trust at all and will share nothing. This time the other person may back away in response to an undercurrent of anger and mistrust. The adult child again feels rejected and hurt. Unable to find a middle ground, she or he will often flip back and forth, trusting completely or not at all. Since it is seldom appropriate to trust fully at first, just as it is seldom appropriate to distrust fully at first, the adult child is engaging in a pattern of behavior which does not allow relationships to develop. In fact, the very idea of a relationship developing one step at a time is often foreign to an adult child. Such ambiguity is extremely uncomfortable for someone accustomed to thinking in all-or-none terms.

All-or-none functioning also affects the issue of personal needs. For the adult child there is no needing "just a little," or "just for a moment."

Instead, he or she flip-flops back and forth between an unrealistic independence ("I don't need anything or anyone") and the opposite stance ("My needs are so overwhelming I can't let anyone know," or, "I need this person so much that I can't live without him or her"). Either extreme leaves the individual's needs unmet.

In terms of the issue of responsibility, adult children of alcoholics vacillate between feeling totally responsible or being totally irresponsible. If they decide they are totally responsible for something, they are also overwhelmed with guilt, because it is usually something bad! They feel horrible that someone missed a bus or that they did not get home in time for some family event. The guilt is all-or-none and generalizes into "All I do is fail." The result is chronically low self-esteem. Because of the rigidity of their thinking, they are either all right or all wrong, and the latter predominates. They rarely accept total responsibility for a success.

49. How can I begin to come to terms with my all-or-none functioning?

Actually, it is a lot easier than you may think. The first and most important thing is to become aware of this tendency. Then, using your hypervigilance, be on the lookout for any extreme positions in your thinking, feeling, and behaving. When you are feeling boxed in or trapped, ask yourself whether or not you could be reacting in an all-or-none manner. Talk to yourself. You do anyway, so it might as well be productive self-talk. And listen to yourself. Only by recognizing your all-or-none functioning will you have the chance to break the reflex. Next, slow down, way down, and take the time to see what options there are, what different ways to proceed are available. You may want to take time out before making certain decisions. If other people are waiting for an answer from you, tell them you do not know right then and will get back to them later. There is great freedom in saying, "I don't know" and, "I need time." Then give yourself permission to talk to people whom you trust and respect. Get help sorting things out. You do not have to handle everything by yourself. Reaching out is a sign of recovery, not of weakness.

Another way to fight all-or-none functioning is to begin making use of a behavior that we call "chunking it down." Chunking it down means taking an issue or objective—such as trusting someone or accomplishing a particular task—and dividing it into its component parts, seeing it in smaller pieces (chunks) rather than as the whole. For example, when you set a goal for yourself, try to identify the different and separate steps that you have to take on the way to accomplishing it.

Suppose you want to be a lawyer. If you are 17 and a junior in high school, achieving this goal will take some time. To serve as a guide for action and to give you a sense of accomplishment along the way, you can break your goal down into a series of steps. Step one is to plan your senior year coursework. Step two is to prepare to take the college entrance exams. Step three is to begin selecting a college. Step four is to get accepted into a college. Step five is to complete each successive year of college. Step six is to get into law school. And so on. Even the steps outlined here can be "chunked down" further. Planning your senior year, for example, involves making an appointment with your school counselor, finding out what classes are required for college, and then registering for them.

As each step is taken, it is essential for the child of an alcoholic to learn to say, "Congratulations, self. You've done another part of it." An inability to appreciate and take pleasure in accomplishing the parts of a task results in chronic feelings of failure and difficulty in completing long-range goals. Only by seeing each step as separate and valuable can a sense of accomplishment be felt and new energy be made available for the next step. Chunking it down helps break the habit of all-or-none functioning.

50. How do I begin to come to terms with the control issue?

This is more difficult. No one will relinquish control until he or she feels it is safe to do so and senses some support. This is why it is important to grasp the all-or-none issue first. The stakes are lowered when control is viewed realistically rather than in an all-or-none fashion. As long as adult children of alcoholics view control as all-or-none, as something they either have or do not have, it will be difficult to do the experimenting required to see what happens when control is relinquished, negotiated, or shared. Seeing control in shades of gray makes letting it go less risky. Before you can let go of control, groundwork needs to be done—not only in terms of all-or-none functioning, but also in terms of building self-esteem. It takes self-confidence to overcome the feelings of vulnerability and insecurity that will initially accompany letting go of control, or acknowledging that in fact you do not have control.

We have been given many unrealistic messages regarding how much we can and should control. Popular psychology often perpetuates the myth of control. We believe that while we can plan for the future, we cannot control it. While there are many things we can control, there are many more we cannot. Sometimes we can control our health, where we live, what we eat, what we think about, or where we work, but we cannot control the weather, the traffic, the economy, what our friends say to us, or what the next words on this page will be. It is a matter of beginning to see that the world really is operating on its own, without consulting us, and people in it are making their own decisions, without our "permission." It is, therefore, necessary to more clearly understand which areas we *do* affect.

Some self-help books stress gaining control of your entire life and creating your own world. While there is some merit to this advice, it is easy to take it too literally and apply it rigidly. Things do occur in our lives that are totally surprising and which we did not call forth. While we believe that it is not possible to control all that happens to us, we do believe that we *can* control the impact events have on us. We can control the way we view such events, how we respond to them, and how we deal with them. For example, there is the fact that you have an alcoholic parent. You did not cause that, you could not control it, and you cannot cure it. But you can cope with it. So while you really have no control over whether your parent or parents are alcoholic, you really can control how you respond to them. One situation that might be familiar to you is visiting your parents' home. If your parents begin drinking, you cannot control their behavior. What you can control is how you respond. Rather than attempting to get them to stop, you may choose to excuse yourself when you see the bottle coming out and say, "Now that the drinking is starting, I'm leaving."

Again, the issue of control is not all-or-none. It is not a question of being so totally in control of yourself, others, and the environment that you can determine what will happen; neither is it a matter of resigning yourself to passively "going along with" whatever happens. Rather it is to acknowledge that there are some things you can control and many things you cannot control. A prayer often quoted in Alcoholics Anonymous and Al-Anon sums this up well: "God, grant me the serenity to accept the things I cannot change, the courage to change the things I can, and the wisdom to know the difference." You can also learn to exercise your right to pick and choose which situations you want to deal with and which situations you prefer at this time not to deal with. Let us highlight that. You really do have a choice about where you want to expend your energy.

If you choose not to expend energy on responding to your parents' drinking, that is an acceptable choice. You may choose not to go to their home at all or to stay only briefly. If you choose not to deal with being around drunks, you can stay out of bars and refuse invitations to parties where there is going to be drinking. Cultivating the wisdom to know the difference between the situations you can change and those you cannot, as well as exercising the choices you do have in dealing with events you cannot change, are crucial in coming to terms with the issue of control.

51. I do not fully trust anybody. I believe others are somehow going to hurt me. What does this mean? Is something wrong with me?

Implicit in this question is the view that even though adult children of alcoholics sometimes appear to give total, indiscriminate trust, in actuality there is an underlying expectation that getting close and trusting others will *always* bring hurt. In all relationships, there is the possibility that the other person will hurt you, consciously or unconsciously, intentionally or unintentionally, even if he or she genuinely loves you. Adult children of alcoholics often have difficulty dealing with this aspect of relationships.

When adult children of alcoholics suffer a hurt, they tend to see it as intentional. They have trouble believing that others did not set out to hurt them and were only acting out of their own humanness. Expecting to be hurt, they may experience another person's actions as hurtful even in situations that could be interpreted differently. They personalize other people's actions. The adult child's all-or-none view and lack of appropriate childhood experiences leads them to think that "normal" family life is supposed to be perfect—everything always works out well and nobody gets hurt. Real life is not that way! You cannot go through life without getting hurt. By the same token, the hurts you experience as an adult do not need to take on the same significance as the devastating pain you experienced as a child when the people you loved the most hurt you the most.

There will always be certain situations in which someone you love will let you down, because he or she does not have the knowledge or the ability to deal more gracefully with that situation. Similarly, please acknowledge the same thing about yourself. There will always be situations that you will not be able to handle well either. That does not mean that you are a bad person or that you do not love the other person. It just means that you are human.

52. How can I begin to work through my trust issues with others?

Change begins with recognition and acceptance. As the child of an alcoholic, you have been exposed to an atmosphere in which you were taught to trust neither yourself nor others. Recognize where your mistrust came from. Know that it served, and can still serve, a valuable and protective function. Understand, too, that you are not bad, sick, or crazy because you find it difficult to trust. Trust is difficult for you because you are an adult child of an alcoholic. Realizing this does not eliminate the problem, but it does provide a frame of reference to help you, slowly and step by step, minimize the adverse effects of mistrusting when you should trust, or trusting when you should mistrust.

Learning a strategy for the development of trust is surprisingly simple. First, you take a small risk. Venture out and say something that is important to you. Stick your neck out a little. After you have done that, pause. Close your mouth; open your eyes and open your ears. Watch and listen to the other person and observe your inner response. Note what he or she is doing and how you are feeling. Suppose, for instance, you have decided to share with someone the fact that you are reading this book and that you are the adult child of an alcoholic. Give the other person the information; then stop, pause, and wait for a response. Watch what the other person does, listen to what he or she says, and become aware of how you are feeling. If you notice that you feel good because the other person says something like, ''How wonderful that you're able to look at those kinds of things in your life,'' or ''I can see that this is an area that's important to you,'' you can draw the conclusion that this person is to some degree trustworthy. Then, if you choose, go a bit further and say, ''Yes, I'm reading this book and one of the reasons that I am reading this book is because I think I may have been affected by my parents' alcoholism.'' Stop. Pause. Watch. Listen. What does the other person say? How does he or she respond? How do you feel afterwards? If the other person now says, ''Oh, how foolish. Why don't you just get on with your life and not blame your problems on your family?'' pay attention to that sinking feeling inside. If you begin to feel as if there is something wrong with you, or you are dumb, or you are copping out, you may want to stop right there and not trust this particular person with any more personal information or feelings.

The example above shows how ''chunking it down'' can help you build trust. Go step-by-step, checking each time to see what happens after you trust a little, and then a little more. That way you can safely and comfortably assess how much, and to what extent, you can trust and be safe with another person. As you "chunk it down," using this step-by-step method of trusting other people, you will need to trust yourself. When you get responses from someone else and try to evaluate them, honor the feelings you have inside. If you begin to feel good with someone or uncomfortable with someone, value that as important information. Regard your feelings not so much as "right" or "wrong," but more as sources of information, ways of attaching meaning to a situation, and learning what is good for you and what is not. Guard against thinking, in an all-or-none way, that these feelings are your only guide, or that they will always lead you in the right direction. Instead, consider your emotions as one very important source of information available to you along with others.

53. How do I begin to deal with my fear of intimacy?

It is probably most helpful if we first define the term "intimacy." Intimacy is the ability to be yourself—who you are, what you are—with another person. The more you are able to be yourself, the more intimate you are. When you are intimate with someone and that person asks you, "How are you?" you stop and think and really tell him or her how you are instead of giving the perfunctory, "Fine." Or you feel free to say, "You know, I really don't want to get into that now." Or, you feel free to say why you feel good, knowing that person will be genuinely pleased for you.

Self-disclosure is a hallmark of intimacy. The more intimate the relationship, the more willing you are to reveal your innermost self. That is why many people are what we call "intimacy-phobic." In other words, they have a tendency to flee as they become more intimate. It is because intimacy is the sharing of feelings, of values, of thoughts, of yourself. To the adult child of an alcoholic that can spell danger. When you become intimate with someone, feelings occur and control becomes an issue. Intimacy can be very scary. It was not safe to be too intimate as a kid. If you became intimate, you might be ridiculed, mocked, or even abandoned. If you cared too much, you got hurt. So as a child, intimacy was dangerous. But that no longer needs to apply. The resources and the experiences you had as a child are quite different from the resources, the experiences, and the situations that you have as an adult. We cannot say that too often.

At this point, one thing that you have that you lacked as a child is real choice. If you do not like what is happening in a situation or relationship, you can leave. As a child you did not have that choice. As an adult, you do. Remember that. It makes a big difference. It means that *now* you can choose to allow more intimacy between yourself and others.

To allow more intimacy, you need to remain aware of your all-or-none tendencies and your need to control. Intimacy does not happen all at once. It is not an all-or-none phenomenon. It emerges in steps and is an outgrowth of a mutual, reciprocal process where two or more people learn not to relinquish control, but to share it. They learn not to give up or grab control, but to negotiate it. At one point, it might be to the advantage of the relationship that person A is in control. At another point, it might be better that person B is in control. At still another point, it might be better if neither is in control.

Intimacy is closely related to trust. In the same way that you might trust a little and then see what happens, you can share something intimate and see what happens. If you like what is happening, if it feels good, you share a little more. If the results continue to be positive, you share more still. The basic strategy therefore, becomes *share-check-share*. This is the appropriate context in which to utilize all those excellent people-sensing skills. Watch, listen, and observe. Know how you feel with this person. Be hypervigilant. Listen to your nervous system. Begin to reclaim its power. Acknowledge your experiences and use your internal responses to help you evaluate what is good for you and what is not. Soon the whole process becomes automatic, and you will not even have to think about it.

Using this strategy, you can reduce major crises in your life because it is less likely that you will share too much too quickly and then be rejected. By taking it a step at a time and avoiding the all-or-none phenomenon, you can avoid situations where you have shared everything with someone who did not welcome it. While it is impossible to avoid being vulnerable when you are intimate, it is possible to greatly decrease the likelihood of being hurt, because you are only sharing a little at a time. By the same token, fear of rejection is minimized because all of you cannot be rejected; only the very small part that was shared that first or second time. If you are rejected, it is only a small piece of you.

For some people, fear of intimacy increases with acceptance as well as with rejection. If your fear increases as intimacy increases, go slowly enough so you will not stumble over your own fear. Create opportunities to work with yourself, and dare to share the very difficulty you are having with some other person. Remembering the strategy, share-check-share, watch his or her response, take a break, and then make other decisions about how much more you want to share, if at all. At this juncture you might say to the other person, "I'm getting really scared. I am feeling that I like you an awful lot, but for some reason it makes me frightened to see you." Then stop. Watch. See what the other person does. See how you feel afterward. All of this gives you more information, more data, more input for you to make your next decision. The feelings that come with being intimate can be frightening. You have a right to experience such feelings and to go at your own pace in dealing with them.

It is also helpful to keep in mind that intimacy is often confused with sexuality. Some children of alcoholics believe sex is all they have to share with someone or that sex is all someone wants. Some mistakenly believe that acceptance of the body in sexual relations means that some major kind of intimacy has been achieved, or that the only way to achieve intimacy is to give themselves sexually. Actually, there can be sex without intimacy and intimacy without sex. There can be a lot of confusion in this area for some adult children of alcoholics who are already prone to confuse feelings.

54. Dealing with feelings is still scary for me. What are some guidelines in dealing with them, especially with the new feelings?

After all that you have been reading, it should be no surprise that dealing with feelings can *still* be scary. After reading this far, you also have some understanding of why this is so. At the same time, you have become more aware of new ways to begin to deal with feelings safely, manageably, and comfortably. We want to emphasize how normal and appropriate your new, emerging feelings are, whether they be feelings of joy, excitement, fear, or guilt. If you did not have them, it would be an indication that you were not working anything through. No transformations would be underway. Your emerging feelings are simply a validation of you as a sensitive, growing person. They are a very natural, very healthy response. Indeed, it takes great energy to block feelings.

Children in an alcoholic home train themselves deliberately, although unconsciously, to be unaware of their own feelings. They survive by denying them. That is what got them through childhood. However, the feelings do not go away; they just build up over the years. As children first learn not to express feelings and soon not to even experience them, they learn to build a wall around their emotions. As a child, it might have really been unsafe to express or experience feelings. Now, as an adult, you have more options, more resources, more choices. Remember that. It is easy to forget.

The overwhelming feelings that you have today will not stay with you unless you invest tremendous energy in ignoring them. It is only when feelings are suppressed and kept underground that they do not change. When feelings are acknowledged, when you become aware of them, you can begin to move beyond them. The very act of expressing a feeling begins the process of transformations.[11]

We must, however, offer a word of caution about expressing your feelings. Just because you have a feeling, it does not mean you have to tell everyone. Be selective about when and with whom you share your feelings. When you share yourself selectively, you will increase your chances of receiving a supportive audience.

It is also important to know that you do not have to do anything about your feelings right now. You do not have to act upon them. That may come as a surprise to many adult children who have learned to confuse feelings with behaviors. Initially, just be aware of your feelings. First, give yourself the freedom to be aware of what is going through your nervous system, without changing the experience itself. After making yourself aware of your feelings, carefully select someone to begin to share those feelings with. Feelings can be dealt with in ways similar to trust and intimacy. You do not have to deal with them in an all-or-nothing manner. It makes good sense to begin to express your feelings slowly, and watch what happens. Watch what the other person does. See how you feel, and continue to use those cues to guide you in terms of whether you want to express more feelings or look for a different person. Again we recommend the strategy: share-check-share. Always give yourself time. For lasting change, the process you go through needs to be done carefully and slowly.

While sharing your feelings you may cry or raise your voice. That is human; give yourself permission to do that. At the same time, remember there is a time and place for everything. When you begin to share your feelings with others, choose an appropriate time. Check with the other person to see if he or she is ready and available to hear what you have to say. Sometimes, even though you have built a relationship of trust by chunking it down and checking it out, it may happen that the other person has so much going on that he or she simply is not available to listen at this particular time. Resist the tendency to take this personally. When your spouse walks through the door after a long day at work, it may not be the best time to share your feelings about the frustrations and disappointments you have had. It might be better to wait until he or she has had a chance to sit down and relax. We do not say this in order to protect your spouse, but in order to protect you—so you can maximize the chance that your feelings will be listened to in a manner that they deserve.

Talking to a professional counselor may also help. Select a therapist with whom you can talk about the issues described in this book. Until you can begin to find out what you are feeling, to accept what you are feeling, and to express your feelings, you will not be able to complete the work you need to do. Words spoken aloud are always more powerful than the words uttered in silence. When a person speaks aloud to another person, feelings are transformed. Communication opens the way for change. That is why it is essential you find others with whom to share. If you have not done this already, you may still be apprehensive, but if you carefully choose the right person and the right time and go slowly, you will discover that sharing your feelings is a very empowering and rewarding experience. It can also be fun.

It is also very important to realize that once you begin to acknowledge your feelings more openly, there will be times when you will, in a sense, "overdose" and decide, "Whoops! That's enough!" and pull back. There is not one straight path to recovery. There will be times when you slip backwards, and times when you just stand still, not sure of where to go next or what to do next. This is normal and natural. If you do not expect everything to fall into place all at once, you will not be disappointed with yourself. Accepting where you are is one of the fastest ways to propel yourself forward to where you want to go. Keep in mind, too, that particularly at first some of the new feelings you are going to be dealing with are really *old* feelings that you have not dealt with properly yet. Those emotions might include rage, anger, loss, and intense hurt. Do not be discouraged or misled if the first feelings you have to deal with are scary, heavy ones. It is only by facing those that you will be able to get to the more positive feelings of joy, happiness, closeness, and self-acceptance that follow.

55. Friends and family are telling me I am getting self-centered. Am I focusing too much on myself and my past?

This is one of those questions we hear repeatedly, particularly as adult children of alcoholics move into their own recovery. They tend to listen to this concern because of their childhood training to consider others before considering themselves. Ironically, people who are truly self-centered and overly focused on themselves rarely pause to consider this. The fact that you even ask this question shows you are still responsive to others' needs and not just focused on yourself. However, it is essential that you take time to look at your needs, your values, your directions, and your goals. All through your childhood you were actively taught not to consider yourself. Now it is time to realize how important you are. One of the main things we would like you to have when you finish this book is a higher level of self-esteem so you can look at yourself, know what you need, and take care of yourself. If in the beginning you are spending more time than usual on yourself, there is no other way that we know of to recover. You must stop and spend some time considering where you have been in order to make the connections you need to go forward.

You also might want to stop and ask the people who are making these statements what they mean. Listen carefully, watch what they are doing, and again evaluate how you feel after you have listened and been with them. Not everyone will celebrate your new growth. When people are involved in a relationship and one person begins to change, the relationship is disrupted.Sometimes that disruption does not allow for the survival of the relationship. This is especially true when the other person in the relationship did not seek the change. The other person gets caught up in a change pattern without necessarily wanting it, or being ready for it. If it throws him or her off balance, he or she might automatically reach out and try to pull you back to the person you were before you started this book and this journey of self-awareness.

If you are like many adult children, you typically do not think of yourself. You are usually taking care of someone else, being responsible for someone else, placating, adjusting, and believing that if someone else is complaining, there must be something wrong with you. Therefore, it should be no surprise that your efforts to reclaim your own boundaries, your own needs, and your own values might be perceived by that other person as a threat, particularly if the relationship is dysfunctional or unhealthy. You might be accused of being selfish or self-centered if you are no longer devoting all of your attention, and all of your time, to your partner. We can only say that we see this as a very healthy, although difficult, change.

One of the messages you picked up as a child was that you really did not have any rights, that you really did not count. You were always second to alcohol. Very early you learned that when you had needs, they would not necessarily be considered by your parents. Your parents may have been in a condition where they really could not attend to your needs. Crises in the home related to alcoholism may have demanded first priority. If you took your needs to your parents and got rejected, you learned to hold back on those needs in the same way you learned to hold back on your feelings. You learned not to share them and not to place importance on them. In fact, if any needs were taken care of, you were the one taking care of your parents' needs.

What we suggest to adult children of alcoholics is that they develop their own individual bill of rights. These rights include the right to personal needs, including time for yourself, the right to your own feelings, the right to your own opinions, the right to decide whether you will meet others' expectations or not, the right to decide what to do with your own body, the right to say no as well as the right to say yes, the right to change your mind, the right to succeed, and the right to make mistakes. You have the right, too, to follow the suggestions in this book or to disregard them. In other words, you have the right to express your own uniqueness.

Having rights is not the same as having a license to do whatever you want to whomever you want whenever you want. There is a difference between "nonviolating expression" (assertiveness) and "violating expression" (aggressiveness). We are certainly not claiming that you have the license to do whatever you think you want regardless of other people. What we *are* advocating is that you have the right to express yourself in ways which do not damage other people. What you will find is that if you do express yourself, if you ask for what you want, then you significantly increase the chances of getting it.

It has been our experience with adult children of alcoholics that they have such an underdeveloped sense of their personal needs and rights that probably the last thing you have to worry about is becoming selfish. If it feels selfish, it may just mean you are finally acknowledging your needs and asking others to respect your rights. When a person has been very non-assertive, for example, it usually feels aggressive the first time he or she acts assertively. You might try out a few behaviors that really are selfish and consider the difference between them and what you actually are trying to accomplish in recovery. By selfish, we mean those behaviors which encroach upon and take advantage of others, which do objectively, concretely, and tangibly impact others in a destructive way.

Remembering the all-or-none phenomenon, it has also been our experience that while some adult children of alcoholics are overly responsible, others are very irresponsible. Some adult children are at one end of the continuum and completely deny all their own needs, while others are at the opposite end. Like the alcoholic in the family, they insist on having their way. They get easily frustrated and do not like it when others are not paying attention. In fact, when these children of alcoholics are confronted with someone else's needs, they tend to either shut down or become abusive. The common denominator in both groups is a severe lack of self-esteem. They really do not feel entitled. They either deny the entitlement or pursue it aggressively for fear of losing it.

It is also true that there may well be times when you do overstate your case or when you do become selfishly demanding. On the road to recovery, you have the right to overstate at times and you have the right to be wrong. No one is perfect. Sometimes you are going to be self-centered and focus too much on yourself and your past. Let yourself make those mistakes while continuing to validate who you are and exploring what you need. If you have been recovering for the last five years, and everybody around you is still telling you, "You're too self-centered, you're too focused on yourself," you might consider whether their criticism is accurate. Initially, as you begin the recovery process, as you begin to make the kinds of changes we have discussed, do not let such reactions from others hold you back. You are not being too self-centered, you are not being overly focused on yourself! If anything, you are probably not being self-centered enough.

We certainly hope that you will feel some excitement and enthusiasm about your transformations, which are leading you to talk about the process of recovery and share much of it with other people. Hold on to that excitement. If you are having difficulty finding people to share it with, find other recovering adult children of alcoholics and talk to them about your experiences and feelings. It is very unlikely that they will think you are being too self-centered or too self-focused.

56. What about this notion of self-esteem?

We have repeatedly said that many adult children of alcoholics have low self-esteem. This is not surprising, given their family backgrounds.

If you think back over what you have read in this book and the memories it may have triggered for you, you will realize that all those experiences of being neglected, of having no one to turn to, of having to be a premature adult, of being told not to trust yourself or your feelings and perceptions foster low self-esteem. As a child, your needs rarely came first. You probably have been given a steady diet of broken promises.[20] You may even have been told that if it were not for you, mom or dad would not drink. In an alcoholic family the child is not the important person. How can children raised in that kind of atmosphere, with so many negative messages, grow up feeling good about themselves?

So yes, unrecovered adult children of alcoholics have low self-esteem. But, they can learn to be more accepting of themselves. The route to increasing self-esteem is epitomized by the title of this chapter, "Transformations." Challenging all-or-none behavior, looking at the issue of control, beginning to re-establish a basis for trust and intimacy, caring for and paying attention to yourself, all lead the adult child of an alcoholic closer and closer to feelings of self-worth, self-trust, and self-esteem. Self-esteem is really the by-product of doing the things that we have been describing. Simply reading this book is self-validating behavior. As a result, you may at times have felt a sense of being more valuable, aware, or intelligent. Take notice of these feelings. Take time to enjoy them. By nurturing what at first are small moments, you can create the space for positive feelings about yourself to grow. Remember that increased self-esteem will be the natural outcome of your efforts to look at yourself and others in new ways.

Keep in mind, too, that transformations typically involve two steps forward, one step backward. What that means is that today you might feel a trace of esteem and respect for yourself, only to have the props knocked out from under you tomorrow. Then you might feel as though you have not made any progress at all. When that happens, reconsider that all-encompassing all-or-none conclusion. Resist the tendency to believe that what is going on now is all that *can* happen. Remind yourself that yesterday you really did feel differently and later you will again.

You might also want to re-evaluate your current relationships in terms of which people put you down and which offer you support. The relationships in which you seem to be getting nicked all the time are the ones that are keeping you in a state of low self-esteem. When you are exposed repeatedly to situations which diminish self-esteem, it is difficult to develop and maintain it. Flourishing in an atmosphere of criticism is like trying to get sober in a bar. It cannot be done.

A woman, who was working in group with us, told us a story that illustrates how subtle negative relationships can be. She mentioned that she always felt bad whenever she was around her sister. One day, when she was sitting with her sister and a friend, our client finally began to understand why. The sister would ignore her consistently, cut her off as she spoke, order her about, and make cutting comments to her. All she knew was that she just did not feel good around her sister. She made no connection between what her sister did and how she felt. It was not until after her sister left and the friend turned to her and asked, "Does your sister always treat you like that?" that this woman began to finally see how blindly she was caught up in a relationship that continually diminished her self-esteem.

To enhance the possibility of increased self-esteem, we strongly advocate that you surround yourself with people who are going to be supportive. In this way you can treat yourself to opportunities to build self-esteem you never had as a child. In fact, you have the responsibility as well as the right to treat the child within you, your inner child, to advantages she or he never had in the past but can now have in the present.

57. How important is it for my own recovery to confront my parents at this stage?

It is very important for you to understand that your recovery does not depend on anyone else's recovery or anyone else's validation of you. This point applies particularly with respect to your parents. You will never see a clear image in a clouded mirror. Your efforts to recover from the experience of growing up in an alcoholic family may be very difficult and threatening for your family to hear about and accept, especially if they are still in the midst of their own survival. Even for many recovering alcoholics, their guilt can be strong enough to make them deaf, dumb, and blind to their adult children's needs.[37] While you will certainly want to acknowledge and address the feelings or issues you have with your parents *within yourself*, the question of whether or not to confront your parents is a whole separate issue. You will need to evaluate whether, and to what extent, talking with your parents about your feelings would be a wise or useful experience *for you*. By now, you are beginning to develop an arsenal of tools and skills for being able to assess whether it is appropriate and relevant to discuss the issues raised in this book with your family.

Certainly, you would not lay this book down, get into your car, drive to your parents' home, sit them down, describe all the information you have been learning, and tell them everything you feel. Instead, you would know to slow down and go carefully, step by step. For example, you might mention that you have a special new book that has been very helpful for you. Stop, listen, note the response you get; note how you feel. Use that information to decide whether you want to say the next sentence. If they ignore your comment and change the subject, the message is probably that they do not want to hear about it. If, however, they indicate an interest in this "very helpful book," you might tell them it is on adult children of alcoholics. Again, stop, listen, note the response. If you feel good about the response, you might then ask if they would like to hear about what you are learning.

As you learn more and more, it may be quite tempting to try to help your parents. Please remember that one of the most important things we know about alcoholism is that you are not going to cure your parents. Your recovery is not going to make them recover. You are not responsible for your parents' alcoholism. You did not cause it and you cannot cure it. You do not owe them the information, and you do not owe them the confrontation. If, for whatever reasons, you think it might be good for you (and that is the key, it would be good for *you*), then you might consider it. Take some time to carefully think over how to approach your parents and why you want to do this. If it is for them, watch out. You are on thin ice and the water is freezing. Your urgency to save them can misdirect your energy. Right now you need your energy for your own recovery, your own healing. That is the only place you can be assured of success. The best thing you can do for your parents now is to attend to your own recovery. If you later decide that you want to intervene on a drinking parent, contact a local alcoholism agency for assistance. You may need professional help.

58. How do I know that I am working things through or that transformations are really occurring?

How do you feel right now? What are you doing with your life right now? Look back over the last several days, weeks, or months. What has been changing? What is different? What kind of messages are you getting from people? Are you finding yourself experiencing new feelings, having new insights? Are you feeling some excitement? Are you noticing that you are less isolated? Are you noticing that you are more revealing of yourself to some people? Or, for those of you who were too revealing, are you finding yourself less revealing? Are you noticing that things no longer appear quite as black and white as they once did? Are you noticing that what has been going on in your life is beginning to make more and more sense to you? Even though you might still be suffering, or confused, and will certainly have backsliding days, are you beginning to see signs of improvement? These are the kinds of questions you need to ask yourself.

We suggest you get out pencil and paper and begin to write down the changes that you have noticed. Save that piece of paper. Display it on your bedroom wall or on the refrigerator door. Do not let yourself lose sight of the difference between where you started and where you are now. It needs to be reinforced over and over. Hang that list up and jot more things down whenever you think of them. Keep reinforcing yourself. Knowing that you are indeed on the road to recovery will help you keep up your energy and your hope.

As we watch adult children of alcoholics go through the transformations process, we have frequently noticed that a new kind of fear begins to enter the picture. While it is fear, it is quite different from the old fear. It is expressed in questions such as, ''When will the bubble burst?''or ''When will the other shoe drop?'' The person asking is looking for a crisis. We often take this as a sign that a person is recovering. Life has been getting more sensible. Life has been getting more steady. If you find yourself with an increasing need to stir things up or to have a crisis, it may be because things have been getting better and you are not used to it. There might even be a sense that things are getting a little boring. Like many recovering children of alcoholics, you may also have the fear that since things have been getting better, you are somehow going to be punished, and you will have to pay for it. It takes a while to accept the idea that you do not have to ''pay'' for feeling good. As a matter of fact, you have already paid the price. You have already paid your dues. And, an exorbitant fee it was! Now it is time to let yourself feel good and appreciate the changes that are occurring.

7

Integration

59. What is integration?

The American Heritage Dictionary defines integration as "the organization of organic, psychological, or social traits and tendencies of a personality into a harmonious whole."[3] Similarly, other definitions emphasize the coming together, the joining, of separate parts into a unified whole. By contrast, dissociation is a separation of parts. When parts are separated from one another, a sense of completeness is missing and confusion is present. There is an internal chaos similar to the chaos in the alcoholic home. When individuals are able to put together the various aspects of their own experience—mental, emotional, spiritual, and behavioral—they can respond to the environment in a more effective way and have a stronger sense of well-being.

As adult children of alcoholics move through the stage of emergent awareness toward core issues and then begin making those transformations which restore meaning and joy to their lives, a very subtle process is set in motion. Adult children rediscover and reclaim the wisdom of their inner experience. Instead of perceiving feelings as treacherous undercurrents in life, they see them as valuable messages. Their thoughts become a gateway through which they can sample life's richness. Most important, an underlying unity develops among their thoughts, feelings, and behaviors. What once were conflicting associations and separate processes now merge into integrated experiences. There is a congruency among them; there is a relatedness among them. It is no longer as if these adult children of alcoholics think one thing, feel another, and do a third. Their feelings, thoughts, and behaviors merge into a whole experience. A by-product of this new connectedness is calmness and joy. This does not mean that problems will disappear. However, it does mean that now they can be handled with more awareness and effectiveness.

Integration is ushered in with the development of a belief system which legitimizes self-acceptance. When the concept of personal rights is understood and adopted, adult children of alcholics are ready to confront the central therapeutic issue—taking care of themselves. They move beyond victimization and see themselves as architects of a new life.

As the concept of taking care of themselves becomes a part of adult children's emerging new behaviors, qualitative changes can be seen. For example, these people may now begin to play and have fun without feeling overwhelmed by guilt. Limit-setting can now occur as adult children establish appropriate boundaries between themselves and others, particularly their parents. No longer tolerant of mistreatment, they find thoughtless behavior in others unacceptable. They can now become appropriately trusting, open to feelings, and are able to make long-term as well as short-term commitments. In group therapy for adult children, integration can be seen when the adult child no longer apologizes for utilizing the group's time.[28] Also, the adult child experiences the freedom—or "personal right"—to answer or not answer another's question, including those raised by the group leaders. The quality of their relationships with others in the group changes in other ways. As group members share themselves more fully, they can allow others to do the same.

One woman's comments during her final group therapy session cogently illustrate the integration stage. All her adult life she had felt compelled to participate in family rituals which had left her feeling exploited and abused. As she put it, "I have spent my entire life being 'the good daughter' so my parents wouldn't be upset by my behavior." She went on to say, "I've learned to be free. Last weekend, I refused to participate in a family activity that included the potential for a drunken scene. I became an adult."

60. Why is integation so important for adult children of alcoholics?

As detailed in previous chapters, the child raised in an alcoholic family is systematically taught to disown his or her sensory experiences. Outer events come to be separated, or dissociated, from their inner meanings. The child is not "allowed" to acknowledge what he or she observes. Additionally, the parents convey the message that the child's thoughts and feelings are "wrong" or "bad." Thinking becomes dangerous, feeling becomes dangerous, and mistrust of one's own judgment develops.

As a result, children of alcoholics are cut off from significant parts of themselves. To survive the chaos generated by parental alcoholism, they are forced to become strangers to themselves, without a sense of "wholeness." Integration is important to adult children of alcoholics because it means they are able to recover parts of themselves that had been lost, and use them to build a more complete identity.

61. I have been reading this book and feel frustrated and confused because I do not seem to be feeling better. Is there something wrong with me?

We have often seen important changes in clients and workshop participants long before they themselves became fully aware of them. There are times when the conscious mind does not recognize its own changes. A familiar example is when someone is drinking alcohol. The objective observer often notices changes occurring in the drinker long before the person drinking is able or ready to acknowledge them. To avoid drawing premature conclusions, you might ask people you trust whether they are aware of any changes or differences in you.

While confusion does not automatically lead to integration, it is characteristic for people to undergo a period of confusion just before they make changes. Confusion is usually a precursor to change and invariably precedes integration. It is logical when you think about it. *Before new patterns can emerge, old ones must be disrupted.* So once again, slow down and watch out for all-or-none functioning as you evaluate where you are now. You might find it helpful to make a personal inventory, a balance sheet, keeping in mind the information you have been learning in earlier stages. Actually record your assets and liabilities, your strengths and weaknesses. Your inventory may surprise you.

Perhaps your perception of no change and increased frustration may be accurate. If you are this far in the book and cannot identify any significant positive changes, examine your own alcohol or other drug use. Ask yourself if it could be interfering with your growth. Just as alcoholics cannot make any meaningful changes until they stop drinking, we believe adult children of alcoholics will not make any significant changes if they are misusing or abusing drugs—be it alcohol, marijuana, or any other drug.

If alcohol or other drugs are not a factor in your life, further exploration is called for. Become curious; sit down with yourself or someone you trust and take stock. It is important to avoid taking an all-or-none stance. You can choose *not* to conclude that being "stuck" proves you really must be bad, sick, or crazy after all. Not making miraculous changes, not becoming noticeably more integrated, may only mean that this particular learning mode—a book—is not suited to you. Different people have different ways of learning. If you seem to be getting nothing from this book, you have discovered something important about yourself—namely that the information offered is not what you need at this point in your growth. You might even congratulate yourself for acknowledging your frustration instead of engaging in denial. Your feelings are not without basis. If you are frustrated or unhappy, your feelings are telling you something is not working. Listen and use these feelings as an opportunity to learn, not as a reason to give up.

If you are feeling discouraged, this may be the time to ask for help. Consultation with a competent therapist, well versed in issues of adult children of alcoholics, might help you if you are still hurting and not making progress.

62. How can I maintain my progress and growth without creating a crisis and without sabotaging myself?

In all probability you cannot, so do not even try! Yes, you read that correctly. Not only will you be unable to prevent yourself from regressing, slipping back, but to do so would be a mistake. Emotional growth characteristically moves two steps forward, one step backward. That step backward provides important feedback. It can provide motivation and opportunity to keep learning. So welcome a crisis here and there. If nothing else, it will remind you what a good survivor you can be when necessary. Life can be unpredictable, which is another way of saying crises are inevitable. The Chinese have an interesting way of forming the word "crisis." It is composed of two symbols, one for danger and one for opportunity. A crisis is indeed the juncture between danger and opportunity. If you view it that way, you will maximize your ability to learn and grow. We, however, are not advocating that you deliberately try to create crises in your life in order to learn from them.

You will need to develop ways to minimize the negative effects of such setbacks. Most important, do not isolate yourself from others when you are in a crisis. To do so will cut you off from their feedback. At this stage your behavior can be very subtle. Friends and family can provide you with important information about your growth which you cannot see.

Beware of all-or-none functioning, be it in thinking, feeling, or behaving. When you find yourself taking extreme stands, seeing things as black or white, and particularly when you see no options, automatically and routinely ask yourself if you are in an all-or-none mode. If you are, search for those shades of gray. If you cannot do it alone, find someone to talk to who can help you.

Many adult children begin to get nervous at this stage because they are not only successful in many of their undertakings but also feel moments of peace. It is the combination of success and peace that can trigger a crisis. Still unsure of your right to success, former negative internal messages may return, saying, for example: "I don't deserve this." Deliberately and consciously replace that habitual message with, "Of course I deserve this!" Not used to the feeling of peace, it is very easy to misinterpret it as boredom or depression. After all, when your adrenalin is not pumping and your heart is not speeding, can you be getting the most out of life? Absolutely! We all need periods of rest and calm.

Finally, make sure you allow for time to think and time to be alone. This will give you the opportunity to consider changing patterns in your behavior. As you spend time alone, also remind yourself, even as you try to make each day count, that there will be a tomorrow.

63. What are the pitfalls in this stage?

This is a very important question. Even in the integration stage, adult children of alcoholics have a reflex toward perfectionism. As much as they have progressed and grown, they find that all-or-none functioning and the need to control fade very slowly. The ghosts of these old habits lurk silently in the background, waiting to re-emerge when the adult child is overloaded, exhausted, or stressed. Integration is not a stage of continual bliss. While there may be moments of utter exhilaration and even ecstasy, the world of the recovering adult child of an alcoholic is not a pain-free, conflict-free utopia.[29] Pain, conflict, and suffering are as much a part of life as pleasure, harmony, and joy. There will always be occasions, no matter how well integrated we become, when life hurts; when life is unfair; and when it just seems overwhelming. That happens simply because we are human.

Many adult children erroneously expect that they should always be able to deal with everything once they start to recover. They assume they should now know exactly what to do with their lives and their relationships. Sometimes they fail to remember that there is no cure for life. They believe they should be able to do anything. In the integration stage, these expectations, assumptions, and beliefs are often very subtle. For example, adult children may make statements or have feelings such as: "Now I know exactly what needs to be done!", "That will never happen to me again!", or "Wonderful, now everything will be okay!" or, "I'm never going to feel like that again!" High on their own sense of potency and actualization, they sometimes forget that while they can plan for the future, they cannot control it. Only by colliding, head-first sometimes, with a limitation, do they understand that they are being unrealistic. However, those who have reached the integration stage soon realize they are being unrealistic, back off, and learn from it. By contrast, in the survival stage they kept bumping into the same limit over and over again, ignoring their experience and denying their feelings. Adult children of alcoholics can get stuck in both stages, but the ways they deal with themselves and others are radically different.

One of the most important pitfalls most adult children of alcoholics face is the way they view the past. In earlier stages of the recovery process the past is seen as the enemy, the source of pain. The past is regarded not only as something horrendous and regrettable but something to get rid of, something to change. There is a big difference between letting go of the past and disowning it.[11] Letting go of the past, which is essential in the integration stage, allows the adult child to move forward without the burden of all those eternal yesterdays. Trying to disown the past, on the other hand, is to deny reality. Denied emotions demand much more energy than acknowledged ones. True integration comes from dealing with both the positive and the negative aspects in life. Integration does not involve the removal of all pain or the elimination of the past. In integration, the meaning and oppression of the past are transformed. As one woman stated during the formation meeting of the National Association for Children of Alcoholics, "This is the first time I have not been sorry to be the child of an alcoholic. It has brought me to this moment in this room with you." In that moment, many different things came together—her past, her present, even her future. Consequently there was a new way to look at the past. Victimization was transcended. Events themselves do not change, but the sense of the experience does. Another adult child stated she never wanted to forget the past for fear she would forget how meaningful the present could be. Only after seeing the tyranny of her childhood, she said, could she appreciate the beauty of a sunrise or truly value being in an accepting, warm relationship which is generally stable, usually predictable, and seldom chaotic.

Another common pitfall in this stage is adult children of alcoholic's over-reliance on one type of experience to the exclusion of others. For instance, feelings which once needed to be denied may now become the primary and sole criterion for evaluating everything. If you feel it, it must be so! Or, newly acquired logical thinking comes to be the sole criterion. Thus, if your reasoning is sound, you must be right. In cases like these, the person's judgment becomes unbalanced. Information which is useful as part of a whole becomes tyrannical and misleading when taken in isolation.

The greatest pitfall of integration is making it something it is not—namely, the end of the effort. Recovery is an ongoing process, not a finished product. Forgetting this leads to an all-or-none stance, to say nothing of pain and frustration. Remembering it gives us the freedom to make mistakes, allowing continued growth and learning. Adult children of alcoholics, like other human beings, always have more to learn. As one poet puts it:

> The journey is never over.
> To travel hopefully
> Is a better thing
> Than to arrive.[45]

64. What are some of the most important processes in the integration stage?

The expansion of one's own abilities and potential requires the same devotion of time and energy that we give to any other important project. Nothing can happen unless we create a space for it. The first key ingredients to effective change, therefore, are desire and commitment. We must make space and continue to expose ourselves to opportunities for growth. We must make recovery important enough to devote our time, our energy, and our thoughts to it. Recovery also requires a clear mind to sustain the work involved. This means that we have to take time for pauses and deep breaths, as well as be free from chemical dependency. The way out of an experience is through it, and our senses must be clear enough to record the journey. We must cultivate the lost art of listening to ourselves. We must learn to reclaim what we once disowned—our feelings, our thoughts, our memories. Self-esteem is enhanced every time we stand up and honor who we are.[12] We must engage in continuous dialogue with ourselves and maintain contact with others. That is how balance is attained, how integration occurs.

Other processes in recovery follow naturally. When we place ourselves in supportive environments, we almost automatically start to learn how to be more flexible in our need to control and in our all-or-none functioning. Our capacity to engage in the kinds of personal and interpersonal interactions that propel us forward grows. We learn the value of exploration and we find that it is much more profitable to investigate than to blame. We learn that feelings are to be regarded as real and important, and we become more willing to express them. We learn that a knowledge of the past is crucial to understanding our present. We learn to share both the positive and the negative, with ourselves and with others. Finally, we learn that our increasing ability to engage freely and responsibly in these new behaviors is healing.

65. How can I continue the process of taking better care of myself?

Continuing to take care of ourselves is a life-long job that only we are uniquely qualified to perform. Clearly, if you have read this far, you have some determination and ability to take care of yourself. Keep reading. Keep learning. When you have finished the last chapter of this book, read more. Go through this book again; review what you might have missed the first time. Look through some of the other books recommended in Appendix A or listed in our reference section. Continue to use other resources like Al-Anon groups or psychotherapy or trusted friends. See these as gifts to yourself.

This is a good time to practice reaching out to others. Reaching out is especially difficult when you stumble and sense those old feelings of being a failure again. Practicing reaching out when you feel good about yourself can make it easier later.

Let yourself continue to make mistakes. Remember, every time you make a mistake, you have learned one less way to do something. Make mistakes and learn from them.

Playing and enjoying life are essential components in taking care of yourself. Many children of alcoholics are required to jettison childhood in order to take on the responsibilities of adult roles. This might be an excellent time to teach yourself how to be a child again and how to have fun. Borrow a kid for a day. Let him or her take you around. Be as silly and curious as you like. Go to a circus, get a bicycle, build a castle or a snowman. A man in one of our groups told us that he did not get a chance to have a childhood when he was a kid. He felt he owed it to himself to provide one for himself now that he could.

Begin to include exercise and a healthy diet in your daily schedule. Exercise is an excellent antidote for depression. It offers emotional and physiological benefits that add up to a new sense of well-being. Try swimming, jogging, biking. Find one activity that you really enjoy. Consult your physician if you have been relatively inactive up to now and be sure to start out slowly. This is an area where you can check your progress on the all-or-nothing front. Is it all right to start off with just a brisk walk around the block? Or do you have to compete in a marathon in your first year of physical enlightenment?

Diet can also affect your moods in subtle but profound ways.[24] Many adult children of alcoholics are affected by sugar imbalances or sensitivities which result in mood swings and "sugar blues." Explore what foods make you feel good and which make you feel bad. Practice some discipline in avoiding foods that are clearly not good for you. A physician or nutritionist might provide valuable guidance here.

Integration is the period when healthy lifestyle habits need to be woven into the fabric of your daily being. If you have been abusing drugs like nicotine, alcohol, caffeine, or marijuana, stop! You do not want to weaken the foundation you have built.

Another crucial component to self-care is listening to yourself, trusting yourself. This has been emphasized throughout the book because of the destructive early training children of alcoholics receive. You are the one and only expert on yourself. You can use others as consultants and books as guides. Nonetheless, you remain the ultimate authority on what you want and need. One warning, however. There are certain areas in which your emotions will lead you back into your personal history. For example, many female children of alcoholic fathers and adjuster or placater adult children of alcoholics feel powerful and immediate attractions to men with addictive personalities. Be careful here. If you start dating a new person and notice that he "drinks a little," do not stick around to see what happens next. You may get stuck. To find these personal "blind spots," do an assessment of what particular decisions or directions have repeatedly turned out to be painful for you. Those may be clues as to where you have unwisely let your emotions override your better sense. If you get confused about this, ask friends who love you if they have noticed any areas where you consistently fail to take good care of yourself. Listen and then decide how to proceed. Requesting feedback in situations like this is one of the ways of utilizing a support group. Surround yourself with competent, caring people who will nourish you.

Finally, we would like to remind you again that recovery is not something attained then forgotten.[29] Additional investments will be required of you throughout the coming years in order to maintain your health and cope with life's continuing challenges. As in any major project, the secret is to work at it one day at a time. Sometimes adult children of alcoholics, like everyone else, tend to get lazy, letting their thinking, feeling and behavior fall into the well-worn grooves of their old survival stage patterns. When that happens, rouse yourself out of lethargy and put into action some of the tools you have gathered from this book and from other resources. Your well-being is much like an investment account. It grows when you make deposits of energy and effort. Good investments earn high interest, and you are your best investment!

66. What resources are needed?

Your primary resource continues to be yourself. External resources available to you include friends, Al-Anon, and various consultants such as psychotherapists, educators, physicians, or even financial advisors. Other resources discussed in previous chapters apply here too, so you might review them now.

We also believe that a sense of humor can see you through a variety of difficulties and enhance your enjoyment of life in general. Consider the drunk who was asked, "Are you trying to drown your troubles?" His reply, "No, they learned how to swim long ago." Such stories allow us to laugh at the truth of our predicament. Adult children of alcoholics tend to take life very seriously, often unable to see or appreciate or even believe in the lighter side. Humor has a way of releasing tension and promoting a more positive outlook. Begin to associate events and memories with humor rather than pathos and drama. When you catch yourself in the middle of one of the core issues again, give a shake of your head and smile at yourself saying, "There I go again! It's another opportunity to learn more about this issue in my life."

67. How can I avoid being "selfish"?

Reread previous sections (such as question 55 in "Transformations") on the issue of being selfish. Pause and take some time to discriminate between "selfishness" and "self-caring." Consider people you know who really are selfish. What do they do? How do they act? Is that what you see yourself doing? Usually, when they stop to consider, adult children of alcoholics find that they are becoming more *self-caring*. Since they are not used to caring for themselves, they naturally feel uncomfortable and worry about being selfish. To check the reality of this issue, listen to what your emotions and intellect are saying as you read this. Then request some input from other persons you trust; evaluate what they say.

We have seen over and over that when an adult child of an alcoholic finally stops always putting others first, he or she is uncomfortable. This is due to the novelty of the situation, and it does not mean the new behaviors actually are very selfish. Self-care is very important. Why not turn around the familiar proverb and say, "Love thyself as you love your neighbor"? A period of deliberate self-absorption is often a necessary prelude to growth. For many people, coming out of years of denial, repressed feelings, and suppressed memories, a time of turning inward is essential and nourishing. Trust yourself!

68. What kind of relationships can I expect to have with others?

We once heard someone say that alcoholics do not have relationships; they just take hostages. We find that this often describes the way the control issue affects relationships of adult children of alcoholics in the survival stage. Because of the need to control, the fear of feelings, and the lack of trust, unrecovering adult children of alcoholics have relationships that require other people to fit into certain strict patterns. As recovery proceeds, relationships begin to allow much more room for individual self-expression. You can more fully reveal who you are in the things you say, do, and share. You can tolerate more differences between yourself and another person in a relationship. The greatest challenge of intimacy begins where the similarities end.

As the fear of intimacy recedes and you increasingly surround yourself with people who respect you and treat you well, your relationships will be fuller. You will hide less of yourself, express more of your thoughts, feelings, preferences, and dislikes. As others reveal more of their thoughts and feelings and as trust builds, you will find yourself more comfortable with differences. You will know that you are not responsible for others or solely responsible for any relationship. You can let others be themselves. Still, sometimes you may feel scared when a friend tells you something he or she wants or does not like. Perhaps you will shut down like you used to do all the time. Such a response is only natural after so many years of practice. It provides yet another opportunity to look at core issues, work on them a bit more, and accept yourself as still growing, still changing, and still learning. In a trusting relationship you can say, "I have to stop right now. I need some time to figure out what's happening with me."

In your relationships you will now also find that when a conflict arises, negotiating occurs more and more frequently. Unlike the conflicts in your alcoholic family, disagreements are typically resolved in a constructive way. Your relationship with your parents or siblings may still not be all you wish. They may not have chosen to recover. Confrontation is one possible approach you might try, but first we would suggest you reread earlier questions in this book about how to deal with parents. Do not set yourself up to fail. You alone cannot determine or control the direction in which your family relationships will go. You may need to let go of your expectations at this point. Letting go allows forgiveness.

On the way to integration, adult children of alcoholics often find old relationships unsatisfying. As they choose to spend less time with some pre-recovery friends, they often fear they will never have any close, supportive friends. It seems to be true that if you are not happy within yourself, every relationship is like a Chinese meal: you are hungry an hour later. However, as you come to feel better about yourself, you have a better chance of developing more satisfying relationships. If new friends are not available yet, take a deep slow breath, pat yourself on the back for your courage (remember, it is not courage if you are not afraid), and remind yourself that good things are worth waiting for. Then plan an activity that is likely to put you in contact with other people who share your interest in self-understanding and a better life. You are ready for fuller, healthier friendships and they are possible. Developing new relationships requires you to be thoughtful, considerate, and sometimes fearful. Relationships take time and effort. Friends are grown, not found. You need to be free to express what you really want and sometimes you will have to risk the relationship to stand up for what is important to you.

It might be helpful to attend a class or workshop on interpersonal communication, or to look for models in your environment. If you know someone who has a happy marriage or a friendship that appears solid and good, watch and listen to what goes on in that relationship. Notice how the partners find the happy side and focus on the good times. Notice how problems or annoyances are confronted, even when they seem scary or petty. Notice, too, how special times, traditions, and private jokes are developed. In good relationships you will see that the persons involved treat one another as valuable, worthwhile human beings. Remember that most of your previous relationships included uncertainty about whether you deserved to be treated well, to be loved, and cared for. Watch out for internal messages saying, "I'm not good enough." Recognize them as traces lingering from the hurts and losses of your childhood. Stay alert to keep those feelings of insecurity from negatively affecting your friends and/or mate. Discuss them when they are in your way.

A scenario of a healthy relationship might go like this:

You are introduced to a person with whom you are to work on a special project. You begin to meet and as you consult on the work issues, your comfort increases and you get around to mentioning a few personal things. The other person responds by taking time to listen to you, supports you in your concerns, and shares a bit about himself or herself. One day you start a meeting by saying you have something else on your mind and cannot concentrate on work—perhaps it is what you are learning and feeling as you read this book. He or she sets the work aside and listens without judging. Afterward, as you reschedule time for the project, this person expresses gratitude that you shared so much and perhaps tells you something personal about his or her feelings.

One day, however, you meet for work and find you were responsible for a major error in the project plans. It will cost both of you a lot of time. The other person tells you how angry it makes him or her without telling you that you are a bad person. You probably feel horrible. All those old failure-oriented, all-or-nothing feelings overwhelm you. You give in to these and maybe even cry. You tell your co-worker you would like to discuss it later, not now. You take the time alone you need to forgive yourself. When you sit down with the other person again, you acknowledge his or her anger, apologize, and together plan to repair the error. You notice that the relationship is still one of respect and caring. The other person still treats you as a competent and valuable person. You have seen that you can handle criticism and that the relationship can survive disagreements.

As core issues are increasingly resolved, through transformations and integration, you will find yourself experiencing more situations like the one described above. Enjoy them!

69. What are my rights as an adult child of an alcoholic?

Your rights are the same as every other human being's. Visualize the person you most admire standing in front of you. Now tell this person what his or her rights are. List them. Now consider the idea that those same rights and those same human privileges are yours, too.

You have the right to seek a happy life, even if no one else in your family understands what you are doing. You have a right to all your feelings. You have a right to be confused. You have a right to not know the answer. You have a right to your privacy. You do not have to tell anybody anything unless you choose. You also have a right to make choices.

In one of the first psychotherapy groups we led, a woman named Sue, the oldest of several children, developed her own bill of rights and brought it to share with others in her group. It was so liberating and powerful that we include it here for you to use as you choose.

PERSONAL BILL OF RIGHTS

1. I have a right to all those good times that I have longed for all these years and didn't get.

2. I have a right to joy in this life, right here, right now—not just a momentary rush of euphoria but something more substantive.

3. I have a right to relax and have fun in a nonalcoholic and a nondestructive way.

4. I have a right to actively pursue people, places, and situations that will help me in achieving a good life.

5. I have the right to say no whenever I feel something is not safe or I am not ready.

6. I have a right to not participate in either the active or passive 'crazy-making' behavior of parents, of siblings, and of others.

7. I have a right to take calculated risks and to experiment with new strategies.

8. I have a right to change my tune, my strategy, and my funny equations.

9. I have a right to 'mess up;' to make mistakes, to 'blow it,' to disappoint myself, and to fall short of the mark.

10. I have a right to leave the company of people who deliberately or inadvertently put me down, lay a guilt trip on me, manipulate or humiliate me, including my alcoholic parent, my nonalcoholic parent, or any other member of my family.

11. I have a right to put an end to conversations with people who make me feel put down and humiliated.

12. I have a right to all my feelings.

13. I have a right to trust my feelings, my judgment, my hunches, my intuition.

14. I have a right to develop myself as a whole person emotionally, spiritually, mentally, physically, and psychologically.

15. I have a right to express all my feelings in a nondestructive way and at a safe time and place.

16.   I have a right to as much time as I need to experiment with this new information and these new ideas and to initiate changes in my life.

17.   I have a right to sort out the bill of goods my parents sold me—to take the acceptable and dump the unacceptable.

18.   I have a right to a mentally healthy, sane way of existence, though it will deviate in part, or all, from my parents' prescribed philosophy of life.

19.   I have a right to carve out my place in this world.

20.   I have a right to follow any of the above rights, to live my life the way I want to, and not wait until my alcoholic parent gets well, gets happy, seeks help, or admits there is a problem.

70. Is there a cure for adult children of alcoholics?

No. But there is recovery. There is no cure because those childhood experiences will always be yours. Those vulnerabilities—genetic, physiological and psychological—will always be there. That is why it is important that you continue to monitor your own drug use and your own adult child issues. There is a human tendency to repeat habits and patterns. It is therefore likely that you will occasionally feel those old "I'm not o.k." feelings. You may also act out those old "I'm not gonna take care of myself or tell anybody" behaviors. When these things happen, rouse yourself again. Look into a mirror and say the things that have had meaning for your recovery. Reread this book. Attend an Al-Anon meeting. Reach out.

Self-monitoring becomes an integral, essential part of your life from now on.[29] A major trauma might still cause you to isolate yourself, drink every night, feel crazy, or become depressed. Watch for those thoughts, feelings and behaviors that are signs of not coping well or not taking care of yourself. There will be other times when things are going so smoothly that you really can just relax and enjoy the scenery on the journey. Take emotional snapshots and create a mental photo album. Make a point of enjoying those times. Trouble, crisis, and trauma are bound to come your way again and worrying will not stop them. So you might as well really relax in the good times and find pleasure in them. They, too, will pass. Then when trouble comes the next time, you can meet it filled with the strength of past joy and happiness, armed with all the resources you now have available to you. Remember—there is no hitchhiking and no short cuts on the road to recovery.

71. Where do I go from here?

You do not need to go anywhere from here, or you can go everywhere. As your self-esteem and confidence continue to increase, you will begin to understand that the main limitations in life are those in your own mind. We do not know what special direction you might take. Your life is unique. We know that in general when adult children of alcoholics reach this stage in their recovery, they say things such as: "I became my own person," and, "I now have the permission to change and the opportunity to direct my life." They write such things as Sue's Bill of Rights. A member in one of our psychotherapy groups recently observed, "Since this group started, three of us have gotten the jobs that we had been wanting for years." Once you free yourself from the chains of the past, turning darkness into light, you are free to go in new directions.

Where you go next is really up to you. You may want to start again at the beginning of this book and slowly make your way through it once more. Or, you may feel you have completed the arduous journey through the first few stages of your recovery and need a break. Enjoy being where you are. Look at where you have come from! Even as you sit reading this page of the book, lean back a bit further, gaze away for a moment, and reflect on all the changes. The next chapter can wait for years, or it may not suit you at all. Either way is all right. It is your choice. As Thoreau stated:

If one advances confidently in the direction of his dreams, and endeavors to live the life which he has imagined, he will meet with a success unexpected in common hours.[51]

8

Genesis

72. What is genesis?

Genesis, in its most basic sense, is the expansion of the body, mind, and spirit, and the developing awareness of a "higher self." It enlarges our vision to fully appreciate the positive, the creative, and the spiritual. Mysticism, philosophy, theology, and now modern science all provide support for the idea of a comprehensive awareness that transcends ordinary, everyday states of consciousness. The promise of genesis is that we have the potential to reach higher levels of consciousness and well-being. We do not have to accept a limited reality; we can actively promote our spiritual development. Through genesis a change in the overall quality of our subjective experience is possible, and a new and varied responsiveness to life can follow.

Recovery from the disease of alcoholism is threefold: physical, mental, and spiritual. Alcoholics Anonymous, the first effective recovery program for alcoholism, has a clear spiritual foundation. We believe that a spiritual side to recovery is applicable to children of alcoholics as well.

We want to share some of our ideas about the spiritual part of recovery. However, we wish to acknowledge that we are, like you, pilgrims on this journey. We also want to share what we have been learning without leading you to believe that there is a specific time frame or pace for your recovery. Neither do we propose a specific belief system. So we ask you to be particularly aware of all it has taken for you to come so far. Remind yourself now of all of the differences in your life today compared to the life you were experiencing before you began the journey of recovery. You are a good and worthwhile person. Your achievements are noteworthy. It is important to start this chapter and the genesis stage knowing that.

73. What can I do to cultivate genesis-like experiences?

There are many paths to spiritual evolution. Those who walk the path of the 12-step programs of Alcoholics Anonymous, Al-Anon, or Alateen travel the spiritual road and, as such, walk in genesis. For an extensive description of the spiritual path to recovery, we recommend Charles Whitfield's thought-provoking and in-depth book, *Stress Management and Serenity During Recovery*[55].

Whitfield suggests the consideration of several principles. The first principle involves "living in the here and now." Living in the "here and now" is often difficult because our mind continually pushes us to live either in the past (often with uncomfortable feelings such as guilt) or future (with equally uncomfortable feelings such as anxiety). To enter deeply into the present moment is to become immersed in a higher consciousness.

Another guiding principle recognized by Whitfield deals with the use of control. Accepting what is, relinquishing control, surrendering to the inevitable, and detachment are techniques which enhance happiness. Alcoholics Anonymous slogans which address acceptance and surrender are: "Let go and let God"; "Easy does it"; "Live and let live"; and "Turn it over." Detachment involves letting go of expectations—the negative or unrealistic expectations which lead to disappointment and pain when they are unfulfilled.

Whitfield also describes a series of practices which can be helpful at all stages of recovery. Many of these have been suggested throughout this book. Expanding your sense of humor, listening to music, communicating with others, being assertive, thinking positively, and taking risks are a few of the techniques which Whitfield recommends. Some individuals also find meditation to be an essential spiritual practice. They find that meditation quiets the mind and opens the heart to higher levels. Prayer and exercise are often combined in meditation.

Many techniques are supportive of spiritual evolution. The choices are yours. As we have said for every stage of recovery—do what feels right for you.

74. Does genesis embrace religion?

While genesis does consist of a commitment to a power beyond one's self and beyond the visible, observable world, it does not require participation in a particular, organized religion. Genesis speaks to universal concerns and is non-denominational. People from all religious backgrounds or from no religious persuasion are free to consider what genesis may offer as a stage of recovery.

If you have been atheistic or unsympathetic toward organized religion, acknowledge your early pain or disappointment. Look at it. Discuss it with those you trust. But do not throw the baby out with the bath water.

Genesis is analogous to the spiritual awakening spoken of in Alcoholics Anonymous; you begin to be aware of a spiritual connection which unites us all in the sense of being one with the universe. Occurring without dramatic flashes of light, we have observed what the psychologist William James calls the "educational variety" of awakening which develops slowly over time.[32]

75. Must I go through the stage of genesis? I feel like I am just getting comfortable with everything I have been learning.

Genesis is meant to complement the recovery process, not compete with it or supercede it. For some, genesis may best follow a period of feeling comfortable with the gains of earlier stages. You do not have to rush into genesis. You are the best judge of what is appropriate for you now. If genesis feels good and right to you, this is a direction you may take. And if you are doing fine as is, you may choose to continue what you are presently doing. As the saying goes: "If it works, don't fix it!" You do not have to explore genesis, but you may choose to.

If you do want to experience the genesis stage, it will take renewed energy and commitment. It does not just happen. We invite you to remain curious and open to the possibilities which genesis offers.

76. If I experience genesis, will I finally get to be perfect?

Alas, there is no perfection even in genesis. While genesis is certainly characterized by deep calm, serenity and even bliss, it is not an all-or-none phenomenon or a continual state of mind expansion. Groceries need to be bought; checkbooks must be balanced; and family and friends die. We simply cannot control all that befalls us. Such a wish for perfection is another example of all-or-none functioning and a common pitfall experienced by many adult children of alcoholics.

77. What other pitfalls might occur in Genesis?

Loss of faith and loss of patience are perhaps the greatest pitfalls. The person who seeks a universal community and consciousness must affirm and reaffirm his or her intent. Over and over the higher choice in each action must be sought. Remember, success can be defined as getting up one more time than you fall down. Persistence is required.

False pride is also a potential pitfall. People who experience genesis are not "superior" to those who do not. They simply are more conscious, more aware. Whitfield[55] makes an important distinction between the higher self (unity, compassion, understanding, and acceptance) and the lower self (power, passion, and survival). If one is preoccupied with the higher self, the lower self may be neglected. The sages say, "Seek Allah, but tether your camel first." To be our higher self authentically, Whitfield states, is to be totally aware of our lower self and take care of it.

To avoid another pitfall, carefully assess your recovery to this point to make sure that you do not jump into genesis in order to avoid the other stages of learning to take care of yourself. It is essential that you have already learned how to attend to yourself and your own needs before you focus upon others and their needs.

It is important not to take this spiritual journey for granted. It must be worked for every day. And when a plateau is reached, treat it as you would any plateau—appreciate the distance you have already traveled and maintain the action that brought you this far. Do not lose faith.

Genesis is a search which can lead you to a lightness that is difficult to imagine until it is experienced. Genesis cannot be forced; you cannot set up a timetable for achieving it. Like a delicate butterfly, if we try to grasp it, we can crush it. To fully appreciate and enjoy it, we must let it go its own way.

78. How do I deal with my parents in this stage?

This is the time that invariably your heart will signal a full forgiveness of your parents. It will be a sense of lightness, freedom from an old burden. Occasionally, this can occur earlier in the integration stage.

You do not need to convey this to your parents directly. You do not need to say, "I forgive you." Rather, begin to think of them gently and wish them well, whether near or far, dead or alive. You may, of course, choose to communicate this to them. However, as we have said before, do not expect them to understand or appreciate what you are experiencing.

79. What now?

As you move along the recovery continuum, you can see that there are no hard and fast lines between the recovery stages. We have also pointed out that progress is not always steady or without setbacks. We believe that wherever you are on the recovery path, you will continue to recover. You will do so at a pace and in a style unique to you alone. There is no recipe or final resting place in human growth. T. S. Eliot says this so well that we end this chapter with his words:

> What we call the beginning is often the end,
> and to make an end is to make a beginning.
> The end is where we start from.[23]

A Final Note From the Authors

What we said in the very beginning of the book is perhaps clearer to you now. You already knew much of what we would say, although you may not have known you knew. The human mind and spirit have many more resources than you realize. They reign over a vast territory of undiscovered potential.

We would like to leave you with one last thought. When alcoholism starts in a family, it moves through the generations. The person who becomes the alcoholic marries the person who becomes the co-alcoholic. Together they have children who themselves often become alcoholic or marry an alcoholic. These adult children will also get married, often to an alcoholic or co-alcoholic. They will have children, and so the cycle repeats.

When recovery occurs, it too is carried through the generations. Everyone has the potential to move through the stages of recovery. And while we each move at our own rate, recovery itself becomes progressive, once started, propelling us forward. You can start a new generation of recovery in your family's history. Know it. Feel it. Believe it. And you can make it happen!

Appendix A
Recommended Reading

Ackerman, R. J., *Children of Alcoholics: A Guidebook for Educators, Therapists, and Parents*, (2nd Ed.). Holmes Beach, FL: Learning Publications, 1983.
One of the first books on school-age children of alcoholics. An early consciousness-raiser.

Black, C., *It Will Never Happen To Me*, Denver, CO: Medical Administration Company, 1982.
A classic on adult children of alcoholics. Must reading.

Brooks, C., *The Secret Everyone Knows*, San Diego, CA: The Kroc Foundation, 1981.
The simple heartfelt personal story of an adult child of an alcoholic.

Cork, M., *The Forgotten Children*, Toronto: Alcohol and Drug Addiction Research Foundation, 1969.
One of the very first books to discuss the needs and issues of children of alcoholics.

Drews, T. R., *Getting Them Sober*, South Plainfield, NJ: Bridge Publishing, Inc., 1980.
A delightfully simple and helpful book for the family of the alcoholic.

Greenleaf, J., *Co-Alcoholic—Para-Alcoholic: Who's Who and What's The Difference?* Los Angeles, CA: 1981.
A classic on adult children of alcoholics. Must reading.

Milam, J. R., and Ketcham, K., *Under The Influence: A Guide to the Myths and Realities of Alcoholism*. Seattle, WA: Madrona Publishers, Inc., 1981.
One of the best books on the physiology of alcoholism. Essential reading for understanding this disease.

Wegschieder, S., *Another Chance: Hope and Health for the Alcoholic Family*. Palo Alto, CA: Science and Behavior Books, 1981.
Written for both the professional and layperson, this is one of the clearest descriptions of the family plight. Must reading.

Whitfield, C. L., *Stress Management and Serenity During Recovery: A Transpersonal Approach*. Baltimore, MD: The Resource Group, 7402 York Road, 1984.
An erudite work. One of the very few to address spirituality and alcoholism. A potential classic.

Woititz, J. G., *Adult Children of Alcoholics*. Hollywood, FL: Health Communications, Inc., 1983.
An important book describing the problems of adult children of alcoholics.

Woititz, J. G., *Marriage on the Rocks*. NY: Delacorte Press, 1979.
Possibly the best book available for the spouse of an alcoholic. Must reading.

Appendix B
Where To Get More Help

Al-Anon/Alateen Family Group Headquarters, Inc.
Madison Square Station
New York, New York 10010
(212) 683-1771

Alcoholics Anonymous World Services, Inc.
468 Park Avenue South
New York, New York 10016
(212) 686-1100

National Association for Children of Alcoholics
31706 Coast Highway, Suite 201
South Laguna, CA 92677
(714) 499-3889

National Council on Alcoholism
12 West 21st Street
New York, New York 10010
(212) 206-6770

National Clearinghouse for Alcohol Information
P.O. Box 1908
Rockville, Maryland 20850
(301) 468-2600

References

1. Ackerman, R. J., *Children of Alcoholics: A Guidebook for Educators, Therapists, and Parents*, (2nd Ed.). Holmes Beach, FL: Learning Publications, 1983.

2. Ackerman, R. J., *Children of Alcoholics: A Bibliography and Resource Guide*. Indiana, PA: Addiction Research Publishing, 1984.

3. *American Heritage Dictionary*, (2nd Ed.). Boston, MA: Houghton Mifflin Company, 1982.

4. Bach, G., and Deutsch, R., *Stop! You're Driving Me Crazy*. New York, NY: Berkley Books, 1979.

5. Bandler, R., Grinder, J., and Satir, V., *Changing With Families*. Palo Alto, CA: Science and Behavior Books, Inc., 1976.

6. Black, C., "Children of Alcoholics," *Alcohol Health and Research World*, 23-27, Fall, 1979.

7. Black, C., "Innocent Bystanders At Risk: The Children of Alcoholics," *Alcoholism*, 1(3), 22-26, 1981.

8. Black, C., *It Will Never Happen To Me*. Denver, CO: Medical Administration Company, 1981.

9. Booz-Allen, and Hamilton, Inc., "An Assessment of the Needs and Resources for the Children of Alcoholic Parents," *NIAAA Contract Report*, 1974.

10. Bowden, J., and Gravitz, H., "Clinical Issue for the Adult Children of Alcoholics," Unpublished manuscript, Santa Barbara, CA: 1982.

11. Brandon, N., *The Disowned Self*. New York, NY: Bantam Books, 1973.

12. Brandon, N., *Honoring the Self*. Los Angeles, CA: Jeremy P. Tarcher, Inc., 1983.

13. Brooks, C., *The Secret Everyone Knows*. San Diego, CA: The Kroc Foundation, 1981.

14. Brown, S., and Cermak, T., "Group Therapy With The Adult Children of Alcoholics," *Newsletter From The California Society for the Treatment of Alcoholism and Other Drug Dependencies, 7(1), 1-6, 1980*.

15. Califano, J. A., Jr., *The 1982 Report on Drug Abuse and Alcoholism*. New York, NY: Warner Books, Inc., 1982.

16. Cermak, T. L., and Brown, S., "Interactional Group Therapy With the Adult Children of Alcoholics," *International Journal of Group Psychotherapy*, 32(3), 375-389, 1982.

17. Clarren, S., and Smith, D., "The Fetal Alcohol Syndrome: A Review of the World Literature," *New England Journal of Medicine*, 298, 1063-1067, 1978.

18. Cork, M., *The Forgotten Children*. Toronto: Alcohol and Drug Addiction Research Foundation, 1969.

19. Cotton, N. S., "The Familial Incidence of Alcoholism," *Journal of Studies on Alcohol*, 40, 89-112, 1979.

20. Deutsch, C., *Broken Bottles, Broken Dreams: Understanding and Helping the Children of Alcoholics*. New York, NY: Columbia University, Teachers College Press, 1982.

21. Diaz, P., "Reaching Hispanic Children of Alcoholics in Their Own Community," Paper presented at the National Council on Alcoholism Forum, Washington, DC: April, 1982.

22. Drews, T. R., *Getting Them Sober*. South Plainfield, NJ: Bridge Publishing, Inc., 1980.

23. Eliot, T. S., *Selected Poems*. New York, NY: Harcourt Brace, Jovanovich, 1964.

24. Erickson, M., *Personal Communication,* Erickson Foundation, Phoenix, AZ: 1984.

25. Fromm, E., *The Art of Loving*. New York, NY: Harper & Row, 1956.

26. The Gallup Organization, *Alcohol Abuse in America*. Princeton, NJ: 1982.

27. Goodwin, D., *Is Alcoholism Hereditary?* New York, NY: Oxford University Press, 1976.

28. Gravitz, H., and Bowden, J., "From Survival to Genesis: A Recovery Guide for Adult Children of Alcoholics," *Alcohol Health and Research World*, Summer, 1984.

29. Gravitz, H., and Bowden, J., "Patterns of Therapeutic Strategies for Adult Children of Alcoholics," Unpublished manuscript. Santa Barbara, CA: 1982.

30. Greenleaf, J., *Co-Alcoholic—Para-Alcoholic: Who's Who and What's the Difference?* Los Angeles, CA: 1981.

31. Hinderman, M., "Children of Alcoholic Parents," *Alcohol Health and Research World*, Winter, 1975-76.

32. James, W., *The Varieties of Religious Experience*. New York, NY: Penguin, 1982.

33. Johnson, V. E., *I'll Quit Tomorrow*, New York, NY: Harper and Row, 1973.

34. Ketcham, K., and Mueller, L. A., *Eating Right To Live Sober*. Seattle, WA: Madrona Publishers, Inc., 1983.

35. Koller, A., *An Unknown Woman*. New York, NY: Bantam Books, 1983.

36. Lilly, J., *The Scientist: A Novel Autobiography*. New York, NY: Bantam Books, 1981.

37. Mann, M. *Marty Mann's New Primer on Alcoholism*. New York, NY: Holt, Rinehart, and Winston, 1981.

38. Martin, J. C., *No Laughing Matter*. San Francisco, CA: Harper & Row, Publishers, 1982.

39. McKenna, T., and Richens, R., "Alcoholic Children of Alcoholics," *Journal of Studies on Alcohol*, 42(11), 1021-1029, 1981.

40. Milam, J. R., and Ketcham, K., *Under the Influence: A Guide to the Myths and Realities of Alcoholism*. Seattle, WA: Madrona Publishers, Inc., 1981.

41. National Institute on Alcohol Abuse and Alcoholism. *Services for Children of Alcoholics*. Research Monograph No. 4. DHHS Pub. No. (ADM) 81-1007. Washington, DC: Superintendent of Documents, U.S. Government Printing Office, 1979.

42. National Council on Alcoholism. *A Position Paper on Alcoholism and Minorities*. New York, NY: The Council, June, 1980.

43. National Institute on Alcohol Abuse and Alcoholism. *A Growing Concern: How To Provide Service for Children From Alcoholic Families*. DHHS Pub. No. (ADM) 83-1257, 1983.

44. *The Network*. A publication of the National Association for Children of Alcoholics, Vol. 1, Number 1, Winter, 1984.

45. Proust, M., *Pleasure and Days: And Other Writings*. New York, NY: Fertig, 1978.

46. Rogers, C. *A Way of Being*. Boston, MA: Houghton Mifflin Co., 1980.

47. Satir, V., (from a poster) *Celestial Arts*. Berkeley, CA: 1975.

48. Schuckit, M., "Biological Markers: Metabolism and Acute Reactions to Alcoholism in Sons of Alcoholics," *Pharmacology, Biochemistry and Behavior*, 13(1), 9-16, 1980.

49. Shain, M., *Hearts That We Broke Long Ago*. New York, NY: Bantam Books, 1983.

50. Steinglass, P., "Alcohol, A Member of the Family," *Human Ecology Forum*, 9(3), 9-11, 1978.

51. Thoreau, H. D., *Selected Works of Thoreau*. Boston, MA: Houghton Mifflin Co., 1975.

52. Vaillant, G., *The Natural History of Alcoholism*. Cambridge, MA and London, England: Harvard University Press, 1983.

53. Wegscheider, S., *Another Chance: Hope and Health for the Alcoholic Family*, Palo Alto, CA: Science and Behavior Books, 1981.

54. Whitfield, C. L., "Children of Alcoholics: Treatment Issues," in *Services for Children of Alcoholics*, NIAAA Research Monograph 4, 1979.

55. Whitfield, C. L., *Stress Management and Serenity During Recovery: A Transpersonal Approach*. Baltimore, MD: The Resource Group, 7402 York Road, 1984.

56. Whitfield, C. L., Personal Communication, New York, NY: 1984.

57. Woititz, J. G., *Marriage on the Rocks*. New York, NY: Delacorte Press, 1979.

58. Woititz, J. G., *Adult Children of Alcoholics*. Hollywood, FL: Health Communications, Inc., 1983.

59. Woodside, M., *Children of Alcoholics*. New York, NY: New York State Division of Alcoholism and Alcohol Abuse, July, 1982.

Index

About the Authors

Herbert L. Gravitz and Julie D. Bowden are specialists in the area of adult children of alcoholics. They conduct training sessions, intensive weekend workshops, individual and group psychotherapy, and educational classes with adult children of alcoholics. They also do research on the topic.

The authors began the University of California's first therapy group specifically designed for adult children of alcoholics. They have presented their recovery continuum across the nation.

Both are founding and current members of the Board of Directors for the National Association for Adult Children of Alcoholics.